Happy Birthday, Kyle

Keep Dreaming...

2/11/90

Peter & Amy

FIRST DESCENTS

EDITED

BY

CAMERON O'CONNOR

AND

JOHN LAZENBY

———

MENASHA RIDGE PRESS

BIRMINGHAM,

ALABAMA

FIRST DESCENTS

IN SEARCH OF WILD RIVERS

Copyright © 1989 by Cameron O'Connor and John Lazenby

Printed in the United States of America

Published by Menasha Ridge Press

First edition, first printing

Library of Congress Cataloging-in-Publication Data

First descents: in search of wild rivers / edited by Cameron

O'Connor, John Lazenby.—1st ed. p. cm.

ISBN 0-89732-079-4

1. White-water canoeing. 2. Rafting (Sports) I. O'Connor,

Cameron, 1953–   . II. Lazenby, J. C. (John Candler)

GV788.F57 1989

797.1′22—dc19   88-9194 CIP

Cover design by Teresa Smith

Text design by Mary Mendell

"China by Kayak," was first published in *Small Boat Journal*, June/July 1987, and is reprinted here with permission of the authors.

"Urban Canoeing" first appeared in *The Washington Post Magazine*, October 19, 1986, and appears here with permission.

'First Bend on the Baro" was first published in *Outside Magazine* in June 1984 and is reprinted here with permission of the author.

"Daredevil Al Faussett" is reprinted from *Does the Wet Suit You?*, Eddie Tern Press, 1981, Seattle, Washington, with permission.

"Rafting with the BBC" was first published in *Outside Magazine* in September 1984 and is reprinted here with permission of the author.

Portions of "Kobuk Solo" appeared originally in *Canoe Magazine*.

Photo Credits:

Cover photograph, Doug Gordon on the Rio Santa Maria, Mexico, by Wick Walker.

Frontispiece: Pakistan's Braldu River flows from the melting ice of the Baltoro Glacier in the Karakoram Range of the Himalayas. Photo by Bo Shelby.

Page ii: Hood River, Canada. Photo by Bill Mason.

Page iii: Below Victoria Falls, Zambezi River, Zambia. Photo by Bart Henderson/SOBEK.

Page v: Photo courtesy Bill Mason.

Page vi: Phil De Reimer near the headwaters of the Rio Paucartambo in Peru. Photo by Mark Allen.

Page xi: Along the Betsiboka River, Madagascar. Photo by Rob Buchanan.

Page xiii: Getting there is half the battle. Nancy Wiley reassembles her kayak in preparation for the Rio Puelo, Chile. Photo by Cameron O'Connor.

Page 165: Lamoille River, Vermont. Photo by John Lazenby.

For Bill Mason, whose spirit runs with the river.

CONTENTS

FOREWORD

My river baptism took place 18 years ago on a three-week journey down the Green. Liz and I rode in a raft with two instructors from Arizona's Prescott College, while seven students paddled in kayaks. It was a memorable trip, and we both fell in love with river running. Somewhat later I took up kayaking, first lightly and then seriously, finally adding this sport to mountain climbing as a principal passion of my life.

I have been climbing since I was 15 years old. I love that sport because it offers a wide canvas upon which to paint adventures, all the way from climbing high peaks to bouldering close to the ground. In climbing, all one needs to be in the middle of an adventure is to find a little cliff, start from the bottom and try to get to the top. If the climb is easy, one appreciates the movement of the body, the texture of the rock, the exercise, and the view. If the climb is difficult, one is quickly pulled into *total focus*—the mind is working, the body is working, and the spirit is working to get up the puzzling piece of rock. The concentration comes naturally because moving around on a steep face above the ground is dangerous if you don't pay attention. In climbing I cherish the twin aspects of keeping risk in control and of facing the unknown. And I love doing things that haven't been done before.

The same elements, I have found, exist in running rivers. Here is an adventure sport that ranges from pure lighthearted play to deadly heartthumping seriousness down steep, roaring rivers. Here too is the fear of the unknown. Danger must be part of it, but the risk must be kept under control by skill and judicious decision making. And in adventure boating there is the opportunity to do new things. The pages of this book record many new things. They record adventure in moving water and that means *rivers*. They tell of magic in that moving water, and its many gifts: gifts of beauty and adventure, of battle and achievement, gifts of joy and of skill, of the pride of mastery, gifts of solo endeavor and of rich companionship. This companionship is another crossover between climbing and river running. My climbing companions of 30 years ago are still among my best friends. And the river-running fraternity includes rare and genuine individuals that I am pleased to call my friends.

The authors represented here form a remarkable company. I am proud to be included among them.

Royal Robbins
March 31, 1988

ACKNOWLEDGMENTS

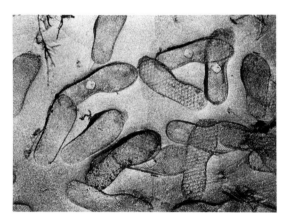

Many thanks to all those who lent an ear or a hand to this project. The book is largely the product of donated efforts. In addition to all the names that appear between the covers I would like to thank:

All the folks at Menasha Ridge Press and Paul Hoobyar, Joe Kane, Michael McRae and Ginny Morell, Kent Ford, Jim Dale Vickery for all his patient and thoughtful communications, Cort Conley, David Bolling, Fletcher Anderson for sticking in there to the bitter end, Christian Kallen and Larry Hewitt. Extra special mention to all those who provided editorial wisdom: Rob Buchanan, Glen Martin, Michael Moore, Ron Watters, Rob Lesser, John Wasson, Standish Marks, Don Banducci, and Allen Steck, who also supplied vintage bottles of Incubus Hills. And for the inspiration that they provided at various stages, I would also like to thank Tom Whittaker, Kim Leatham, Nancy Wiley, Kevin Padden, the Washington Kayak Club, and the Nahanni Crew, who got me started.

Cameron O'Connor

A first descent is the quintessential river experience: unknown obstacles, the demand for teamwork, the pressure of do-or-die decisions. In addition to the glory of being first, there is a sense of accomplishment from overcoming seemingly insuperable difficulties. More importantly, there is a personal sense of discovery and the shared bond of comradeship.

In the past 20 years, river exploration has lured boaters to the far reaches of the planet, from Papua New Guinea to Ethiopia and Iceland, as well as to unrun streams in their own regions. In the effort to chronicle recent first descents, the media tend, inevitably, to focus on the most difficult, the longest, the fastest, the most treacherous rivers. Sometimes, though, the heart and soul of the sport seem to be lost in the fanfare of the elite first descent, in the pounding noise of helicopters bearing film crews, and in the intonations of television narrators. Amid the superlatives, the basic attractions of river running, the things that continue to draw people to rivers again and again, may be obscured. And there are many, many first descents of a particular river, because one occurs each time someone who has never been down that river pushes off from the bank, and each time a paddler rediscovers a river he or she has paddled many times before.

So we chose the excellent stories that make up this book because they portray first descents in a broad sense. We chose them for their excitement, but also for their humor and for the insights they provide into why we run rivers. What they have in common is the thrill shared by all who run a river for the first time.

They range from William Nealy's backyard boyhood adventure in a rain-swollen Alabama creek to Andrzej Pietowski's tense, almost religious passage through the deepest canyon on earth; from Jeff Rennicke's soulful solo trip on Alaska's Kobuk, to the pure exuberance of Peter Skinner's run of the Niagara Gorge and of Chuck Stanley's first descent of California's Bald Rock Canyon, made with a 1956 VW bus as base camp and a ten-speed bike for a shuttle. David Roberts examines the combination of television and the big-time first-descent expedition; Bill Mason experiences the lure of an unrun canyon near the Arctic Ocean; William Scheller slogs through the phlegmatic suburban waters of the Anacostia, and Robert Portman and Dan Reicher explore China by boat. There is Richard Bangs's rich remembrance of discovering the Colorado and river running as a young man, Galen Rowell's photo essay on the Karakoram's challenging Braldu River, and, from the imagination of Timothy Hillmer, "The Hookman," a fine short story.

There are these stories and more, stories from Africa, Asia, and South America; from Canada, Mexico, the continental United States and Alaska. These are often tales of challenge and reward, of risk and loss, and, in more than one account, of death. They don't address river safety or river conservation per se because these crucial issues are best dealt with elsewhere. The reader should keep in mind, however, that many of the activities described were undertaken by expert paddlers with years of experience.

In each of these stories the author speaks with a different voice. But all of them exemplify the many levels of river-running adventure. At the bottom of each is the almost mystical lure of rivers that Pietowski describes in his tale of Peru's Rio Colca, which opens the book. We hope that *First Descents* will be, like moving water wild or smooth, an invitation to the world's rivers and, like those rivers, a rich and continuing source of pleasure, respite, and discovery.

IN THE BELLY OF THE EARTH

By Andrzej Pietowski   Translated by Dark Oglaza

Perhaps George Mallory characterized the sensation best when, asked why he had set sights on then unconquered Mt. Everest, he replied, "Because it was there." His terse, seemingly whimsical answer is now legendary—perhaps because it symbolizes the quasimystical lure that the unknown, the unconquered, has on all of us. Looking back on the events that led me and my companions—then residents of Cracow, Poland—to the Colca Canyon in the Peruvian Andes, I get the impression that a similar mystical spirit was at work. But unlike Mallory, who found himself drawn toward the crest of the world, we were lured to the deepest canyon on the planet, the belly of the earth, from which cliffs rise more than 10,000 feet.

At first all we had to go on was the suggestion of my friend Piotr Chmielinski—who later became the first man to kayak and raft the Amazon from its source to the sea—that we explore a number of rivers in South America. The idea appealed to us immediately. At the time we were completing our studies in Cracow and I think we all sensed that an era in our lives was coming to an end. We would soon have to accept the "adult" responsibilities of work and family; in short, though we felt confident in our abilities—we had had by then extensive river experience on our native Dunajec and also in many other parts of Europe

On the Colca, self-rescue is *de rigueur*. Even a helicopter can't help you here. Photo by Andrzej Pietowski.

—we also realized that the moment was at hand for an exceptional adventure. It would be now or never, but where to begin?

In Poland, to even mention that we were planning to explore a river in South America was grounds for institutionalization. Along with the customary obstacles one faces while preparing for such an expedition—plotting courses, gathering supplies—one also has to take into account any number of political obstacles. Poland is, after all, behind the Iron Curtain, with all the attendant problems. Similarly, the political upheavals that constantly plague much of Latin America further complicate matters, a fact well illustrated by the many problems we encountered obtaining entrance visas.

Our first contact with the Colca came in 1978 when we came across an article describing the region. It had been written by Professor Jose Arias, a Spaniard who had developed an interest in the river based on the work of a colleague, Professor Gonzalo de Reparaz, who lived in Lima. The canyon itself was first "discovered" in 1929 by two American airmen who had cleared a small airstrip and flown several exploratory missions over the canyon in a single-engine plane. The airstrip was near the place called the Condor's Cross, where we would later begin our journey.

The entire region was largely uncharted, despite the fact that during the Inca Empire, the Colca River Valley was a vital and thriving center, laced with a network of irrigation channels. Even today one can make out remnants of steep stairways cut into the bare walls of rock, the famous Inca Trail that was used to move armies from one corner of the empire to another, as well

as to transport fresh fish from the Pacific to remote Andean areas.

Reparaz, we later learned, had had a keen interest in the canyon for several decades. His interest in the Colca was contagious. In 1978 Doctor Arias as well as Professor Max Weibel of Switzerland made their own cursory explorations of the canyon. Still, their party hadn't included any experienced river runners and thus almost the entire canyon remained unexplored.

Once our initial, vague plans of running rivers in South America crystallized, we set our sights first on the rivers of Argentina. No sooner had we done so when, because of a dispute with the Chilean government over a number of small islands in the Beagle Channel, the Argentine government summarily revoked our visas. We then changed our plans, looking toward Peru and its rivers, especially the Colca.

Already booked on a ship out of Gdynia, we found another unexpected obstacle. This was in the winter of 1979–80, the one winter in a hundred when the Baltic froze. We resigned ourselves to waiting until the sea was once again navigable, but then the military junta governing Peru abruptly revoked our visas. For the first time, after two years of exhausting preparations, we talked of giving up the whole affair. Still, we went on, now looking toward Mexico. As luck would have it, the government there granted us visas almost immediately.

We arrived in Peru in February, 1981, via Central America, but we still didn't have a clear idea of how to approach the Colca. The river was there, so were we, but we had little else to go on. It was then that we happened to meet Professor Reparaz himself. He asked us to stay in his home in Lima and, once there, allowed us to examine all of his maps and diagrams. He also infected us with his fascination with the Colca. He was enthusiastic and encouraging, yet we sensed his apprehension about the risks we would face.

It was on May 13, 1981, in a small Andean village, Chivay, 3,600 meters above the Pacific Ocean, that we first heard of the attempt on the life of Pope John Paul II. We managed to get our hands on a battery-operated radio and, in the night's cold—our tea freezing up in our canteens—we listened silently to news bulletins coming across in what seemed all the world's languages. Looking back on it, I believe we formed a pact in the silence of the night. In short, any of us who still might have entertained doubts about taking on the canyon dropped them then and there.

To understand what the death of John Paul II meant to us—we inferred from those early communiques that he had been killed—I suppose you would have to be Polish. Here was the man who had been raised and later served as a priest and a bishop in our home town, dying at a pivotal moment of our nation's history. And I now realize that perhaps much of our resolve to go ahead, to take on the canyon, was a kind of self-defense. We believed that through physical exertion we might get our minds off the tragedy unfolding half a world away.

At this time, Solidarity, the movement that had arisen in and spread through all of Poland, seemed to be altering the state of things not only in our homeland, but in a good part of Europe as well. Since we had left Poland we had heard stories about its ascendancy from broadcasts and from sailors, and, to tell the truth, we felt like

deserters. But that wasn't unusual considering that, given our nation's history, its shocks and misfortunes, a tradition of social responsibility has become quite pronounced. And it was in the spirit of answering for our actions, I'm sure, that we decided to go on with our plans, to do what we knew best; in short, we would run the Colca, conquer the unconquered.

The next morning, still believing that the pope had been killed by an assassin's bullet, we took a brief, exploratory excursion down to the mouth of the canyon. The river seemed shallow, uninviting. But, by then, it seemed nothing could dissuade us from continuing.

Judging from the charts Reparaz had shown us, the first stretch of the journey would be the most difficult. Here, we faced 44 kilometers of uninterrupted river with no hope of turning back. At the end was a small Indian village, the Canco. From there we had another 56 kilometers to go, though this second stretch, unlike the first, was punctuated with gorges and tributaries that made it possible to leave the canyon. In spite of the fact that the first stretch sloped approximately 800 meters—and this no smooth gradient but a rough course of sudden, sharp falls and cascades—we believed we would finish it in five days.

Looking back on it, I'm convinced that no American explorer would have even glanced at the Colca had his party been as ill-equipped as we were. We had two rather flimsy kayaks, a smattering of pine paddles which, through the run, snapped like so many match sticks. Our headgear consisted of Soviet hockey helmets. No one had brought a waterproof camera, nor had anyone thought of bringing along a radio. Our most valuable possessions, our movie camera and

The Colca Canyon in southern Peru is the world's deepest; the path to the
Rio Colca is as arduous as the river itself. Photo by Andrzej Pietowski.

other photographic equipment, we wrapped in
sheets of plastic, convincing ourselves that these
were waterproof. Our raft, on which we would
pile all of our supplies — a weight of about 500
pounds—was a good one. But worst of all, we
hadn't brought any warm clothing, reasoning
naively that, after all, Peru has a warm climate.

It was no wonder that, when we packed our
supplies and returned to the mouth of the canyon, the German backpackers we met there exam-
ined us suspiciously. No wonder when they
learned we were about to run the river they began

snapping photographs of us, as if we were some
peculiar natural formation.

Our first day out was idyllic. We made about
eight kilometers, photographing and filming at
our leisure. We moved haltingly. The canyon
walls at our sides rose three to four kilometers
straight up above us, the rock striated, eroded
heavily. The landscape, barren and unearthly,
reflected an ongoing geological process that probably had begun 10,000 years before with the erup-
tion of a volcano near present-day Arequipa—an
explosion that threw into the air a million tons

of rock, dust, and lava and subsequently covered the riverbed. Slowly, the river, undaunted, began to break up the thick layer of rock, pushing it out into the Pacific. The signature of this process is found in the striation. Avalanches are common every year, during the rainy season. The settled debris often dams the river, leaving a series of natural lakes. It doesn't take long, though, for the river to push past these dams, to carry the debris out into the Pacific, and in doing so, to pound out new openings in the canyon walls, hence creating new channels along the length of the canyon.

Inside, it's beautiful. One canyon wall is brightly lit, the other left in deep darkness. The temperature difference accounts for the strong air currents that wind through the canyon. They kicked up spray in our faces, at times holding our raft still despite the river current.

Piotr and I are out in front in our two kayaks, like scouts. We stay ahead of the raft, feeling the river out, testing approaches, anticipating rough spots. The kayaks are truly indispensable. They even tow our raft when necessary. And I'm sure we both had every intention of staying in them throughout our run. After all, unlike the raft, a kayak gives one a feeling of safety—its maneuverability promises quick escape, its frame a buffer against the river.

On our second day out our raft overturned suddenly in what seemed a relatively easy rapid. It floated upside down towing the raftsmen behind it right through progressively stronger currents. Reaching down from my kayak, I managed to grab hold of a line and, bracing against a boulder, pulled the raft toward the bank—effectively grounding it. It took me a second to realize that the raft had been towing only three raftsmen and

The canyon walls record the geologic history of the earth. Photo by Andrzej Pietowski.

that our fourth, Stefan, was missing. I paddled upstream quickly, blindly, until I finally spotted a yellow helmet, then a red vest, and Stefan himself, naked from the waist down—the force of the water had torn his pants and shoes right off. He was hanging precariously from a rock under a cascade, red-faced but intact.

That was the first lesson. Our second came two days later, on our fourth day out, when the kayak I was paddling was wrecked in the rapids. We hadn't brought any resin with us to repair the damage so, sadly, I left its corpse on an outcropping of rock and took my place in the raft. No safety there. No buffer.

The days passed quickly. We grew more and more tired, realizing that our estimate of five days was way off the mark. Many cascades were simply too risky and we ended up portaging our supplies around them. In addition, the river widened at points to about 20 meters and narrowed to as few as 3. At times, our raft was caught between boulders and took in water while we frantically tried to work it back into the current. I was afraid to even think of what would happen to us if the raft were punctured or if we lost our other kayak.

The landscape was truly dazzling. Somehow, I find it impossible to describe—no totally suitable metaphors come to mind. Perhaps "mythical" and "primordial" come closest. Later, on a subsequent trip, we would take a number of geologists with us through the Colca and they wouldn't be able to take their eyes off the canyon walls—those living testaments, those striations that impassively wear the history of our planet's formation. Era after era. Age after age. Period after period. Unlike those geologists, I took a more active interest in the many rock towers thrusting out from the river, stretching for kilometers at a time, seemingly frozen in space. A number of these resembled sculptures. I made out a child's head in one, a camel in another and, the most mysterious, a remarkably intricate castle with two rocky towers.

Often we spied steam rising from a hot spring. Geologically, the area is full of activity, despite its barren appearance. One familiar element was the strip of blue we saw above, very high up, but too often it took on a strange character, dotted more and more with the craggy silhouettes of condors.

It was on our fifth day out, after a particularly grueling experience portaging our supplies around a cascade, that the stark reality of our situation dawned on us. By three o'clock the sun dropped behind the peaks to our right, it grew cold and we decided to bivouac. Our clothing, light as it was, was sopping wet. Hanging our supplies out to dry, we fixed supper from the assortment of powders and dried goods we had brought along—mixing them in a large kettle. Our fuel had long since given out and we had to resort to gathering whatever sticks we could find for a fire. It seemed that nothing grew along the Colca—for five days we hadn't seen a single scrap of vegetation—and we knew that we would have to rely on our own provisions. But this had been measured out with a druggist's concern for quantity, and it was on that day, wet, tired beyond belief, that we realized that if we didn't pick up our pace we could simply die of hunger.

Our talk, as it often did, turned to food. Someone reminisced about some wonderful pastries he had had at a hotel in Cracow. Talking about food seemed our favorite pastime, besides, perhaps, keeping our eyes fixed on the sheer walls above, whenever we stopped, watching for the first signs of an avalanche. A minor tectonic nudge would have meant the end of us.

During that time, two dreams kept recurring in my sleep. In the first, we are being buried in an avalanche and in the second I'm drifting down river and unable to stop, and I can hear the roar of a waterfall, growing louder at every instant. My companions reported similar dreams.

As time passed, the condors grew more and

Nightmare come true: because of the Colca's sheer walls, some drops had to be run without scouting. Photo by Andrzej Pietowski.

more daring. Our only consolation was that if we died these huge birds would hardly have made a meal out of the six of us; we looked like walking skeletons.

After the fifth day, the rest blur together in my mind. The sameness of those days: holding the damaged raft back with all our might while it dances at the top of a falls, carrying our supplies around, making camp, breaking camp, dreaming of avalanches, filming the scenery, noting silently the beauty of the vista revealed past the bend in the river, anticipating danger, the relief of seeing it pass. . . . Skinned knuckles. Sunburn. Our jokes, our conversations. Monotony.

We never spoke of those things closest to us. We never mentioned the most important things. The coldness of the night. Doubt. Faith. The meaning behind experiences. We never spoke; it was still too soon for these matters.

On the tenth day, we spotted a number of hills resembling those we had seen in the photographs taken by Jose Arias—eroded hills marking the location of some waterfalls and then, hopefully, the first settlement.

On the eleventh day, I recall the three cascades over which we carried our supplies on our backs. It was probably the single most fatiguing part of our journey—our Calvary. Suddenly, I spotted vegetation in the distance, beautiful clusters of green. Is it a hallucination? No, it's real. The end of the canyon. "Land, land," I called to my companions.

We drew closer with what little strength we had left and landed on a small rocky beach. We immediately noticed that behind the foliage beyond, eyes were examining us suspiciously. We understood their fear. These Indians, direct descendants of the Incas, have a marked aversion to water. It is believed that none of the ancient Incas knew how to swim—their mythology included a wealth of river demons. Some of these beliefs apparently persist today. More than once we noted that Andean Indians, leading a herd of llamas home from the other side of the river, would not cross a footbridge after sunset—rather they would make themselves comfortable on the other side, wrap their ponchos tightly around and wait patiently for sunrise. Now, confronted with six strange-looking bearded whites approaching from a side no one in their recollection had ever approached from, they were startled. They had reason to be afraid.

We removed our helmets slowly and called to the Indians in Spanish. This settled their minds. Where are we? In the Canco? Right, right in the Hacienda Canco! We are saved!

They greeted us warmly then, bringing food, as other Indians had centuries before to Christopher Columbus on the shores of America. Whether this was to placate us or if it was because we were so wasted away from hunger, I can't say. There was sweet corn, a white cheese and, in the settlement where they had led us, eggs. Enough so that we had two each.

Later that evening we got our hands on a newspaper, only a few days old, and discovered only then that the pope had survived. Out of all the joy we felt in that moment we spontaneously named those great waterfalls we had portaged only that morning after John Paul II. Then, we

A rock-strewn cave provides a calm refuge from the cold evening winds. Even accommodations like these were hard to find. Photo by Andrzej Pietowski.

also found a bottle of whiskey in our supplies (whether it was left to celebrate just such an occasion or reserved as a buffer against a worse fate, again I can't say for sure) and drank to our new Indian friends.

After a ten-day rest during which we made repairs, the second 56 kilometers of our journey took us only five days. The terrain was kinder and we were delighted that the turquoise water of the Mamacocha covered boulders in the river, making our journey that much easier and faster. We relaxed, subsequently, and letting down our guard, we were nearly killed in what turned out to be a very beautiful waterfall. Ironically, we named it after Professor Reparaz. Then, everything came to an end. Suddenly, the canyon walls drew back as easily as a theater curtain. The river ran along a flat surface straight to the Pacific. We have a few photographs in which we're making faces at the camera. Was it over? The end? We look worn out, our clothes in shreds.

Before we knew it, we were at the press conference: photographers, microphones. Suddenly our pictures were in the newspapers. We were on TV. People wanted to touch us; they were calling after us. We had an audience with the president of Peru.

Where were we in all of this? What I remember most is one fleeting moment when, floating out of the canyon, we all turned back for a last look, as if we wanted to call back those endless, vertical walls that had towered over us for almost a month. Suddenly, I experienced the feeling of longing, longing for the canyon. It was almost as if we had left something back there—something viable, breathing, some small but living part of ourselves. That longing has remained within me ever since. For this canyon, for another, maybe still unconquered one.

METAMORPHOSIS

By Richard Bangs

I conned my way onto the Colorado. In 1968, with no background as a river guide and no rafting experience, I composed a letter to Ted Hatch, one of the Colorado River raft concessionaires, asking for a job. I lied through my teeth. I had never rowed the Green —in fact, I had never ventured west of the Blue Ridge Mountains in my wan 18 years—but I said I had, in elite type with a carbon copy. I even fabricated a few canoe races I'd won and crafted a fake letter of recommendation from the president of my canoe club. I let my moral compass spin and point west. I wanted to float that special canyon that lined a fifth of the Colorado River's 1,400-mile course from the Rockies to the Gulf of California, and I was willing to do most anything to get there.

It began with the monthly meeting of the Canoe Cruisers Association of Washington, D.C. I was a recent high school graduate searching for life's passion. I had joined the cruisers at the urging of my scout leader and was immediately hooked. Canoeing consumed my summer weekends. I broached Grummans and splintered white ash paddles on the Chattooga, the Nantahala, Youghiogheny, Monongahela, and Potomac. Then, at the meeting that would change my life, the main event was a film of members who had canoed, in special decked models, the Colorado River through the Grand Canyon, outfitted by Ted Hatch.

As the images flickered, a spell was cast. The Colorado's waves seemed oceanic, ten times the size of anything I'd encountered on the Cheat or

A Colorado River guide is inextricably bound to the mystique of the Colorado River and the Grand Canyon. Mike Vering rows a calm stretch above Fossil Rapid. Photo by Curt Smith.

the Rappahannock. The scale of everything was overwhelming: the canyon walls, the crests and troughs, the eddies, the wet grins. Some ethereal hand reached from the screen and pulled me in. Destiny beckoned, and I drove home with a monomaniacal craving: I had to run the Colorado.

Hence my missive to Hatch, a resume Nathaniel West would have appreciated: rafted 22 major rivers, guided professionally for three years, knew all the ropes (when in fact I couldn't even tie a bowline).

But it worked. In 1968, the rafting business was barely that, although rapid growth was just around the bend. Bobby Kennedy had floated the Colorado with Hatch the year before, and the story had gone around the world. Suddenly, rafting the Colorado was in vogue. Hatch had to meet this growing demand with more crew but had few prospects. The career of river guide just wasn't widely known beyond Page, Arizona, and Vernal, Utah, and Hatch already had the best and the brightest from each in his employ. So he took a chance on me, sight unseen. "Report to Lee's Ferry April 28 for a trip departing April 29. Welcome aboard," he wrote, words that fueled me through six cold months of school.

The flight into Page over the southern rim of the Colorado Plateau was spellbinding. I'd never seen such an expanse of uninhabited land, gaunt and devoid of almost any sign of man. In the soft coral flush of daylight, I pressed nose against window in awe of the beauty below. No landscape ever appeared so dramatic, so operatic. Then, like a giant gash in the skin of the desert, it appeared: the canyon of the Colorado, a dark, crooked rip tearing into the horizon. In the middle distance were the Vermillion Cliffs, living up to their name.

Circling over the Glen Canyon Dam, the 600-foot-high plug that creates 180-mile-long Lake Powell, we started our descent into Page, a town erected in the dust of nothingness in 1956 to accommodate the dam workers. Here, at the Page Boy Motel, I found Ted Hatch, a rotund redhead whose father, Bus, had pioneered many rafting runs in Utah and Colorado in the thirties and forties. He extended a freckled hand in greeting, but couldn't mask his disappointment as my skinny hand met his. He had hired a gangly, pale easterner who appeared as guidelike as Ichabod Crane. But he rolled with it.

"You're swamping tomorrow's trip," he said. "We have the Four-Corners Geological Society, 110 people, ten rafts. Drive the winch truck down to the Ferry as soon as you change out of that blazer and help the boatmen rig. Welcome aboard, kid."

"Ahh, one question, Mr. Hatch."

"Call me Ted . . . what's that?"

"What's a swamper?"

Ted's cabbage-patch doll head reared in laughter before he explained. "You dig the toilet hole at camp, help the boatmen cook, wash the dishes, bail the rafts, and assist the guides in every way. Now get on it."

He handed me the keys and pointed to the truck. When I sidled into the cab, I knew I was in trouble—it was a stick shift. I'd grown up in an automatic suburb, had never been in a car with a manual transmission. Still, I knew the basics. Toeing the clutch, I maneuvered the stick into first and eased forward. Beautiful. I headed down the motel driveway, a wave of pride washing over me. I slipped into second. No problem. Then, a thunderclap, and plastic shrapnel sprayed the windshield as the truck jerked to a halt and

Skirting "Land of the Giants," an oar rig blasts through Crystal Rapid.
Photo by Curt Smith.

stalled. I leapt from the cab and surveyed the scene. I had driven the truck winch, which stood a good five feet above the cab roof, smack into the middle of the Page Boy Motel sign hanging above the driveway. Roaring obscenities, the motel owner bolted to my side with Hatch in tow.

"Can you take it out of my pay?" I asked Ted meekly.

"Forget it, kid. I'll cover it. But don't screw up again."

Somehow I managed to get the truck down the 50-mile route, over the 470-foot-high Navajo Bridge, to Lee's Ferry, one of the only two road-access sites for the length of the canyon.

And such was the beginning of a miraculous metamorphosis—from sandstone to schist, boy to boatman, river novice to river god.

Lee's Ferry is mile zero of the 277-mile Grand Canyon experience, the launching pad for all river trips. I wheeled down the ramp, where a line of 33-foot-long World War II surplus pontoon bridges, refitted as passenger-carrying rafts, were being inflated using gasoline generators. Stepping out into the searing 95-degree heat, I faced my colleagues-to-be, and encountered river guides for the first time. Ten of them—bronzed beyond belief, muscles defined like Rodin sculptures, hair thick and bleached by the desert sun. One guide sported a tattoo of a fly chasing a spider.

All seemed several inches taller than my six-foot frame and 30 pounds heavier, all gristle, sinew, and barely bridled power. As I made the rounds of introductions, I felt as out of place as a white-tailed deer in a pen of Brahma bulls. Not one spoke with the enforced sense of grammar and syntax that had filled my upbringing. All were from the West, where a different value system prevailed. Here, style, smile, and tan made nobility.

I was assigned to the cook boat, piloted by 26-year-old Dave Bledsoe, a black-haired bear of a boy, son of a Lake Mead marina manager. We would precede the ten-raft flotilla to each camp and set up the commodes—I was a quick general in this one-man brigade—and the kitchen. Each morning, after the five-score and ten geologists departed on the other rafts, we would linger to clean up camp and bury the mountain of trash and excrement. This was long before the enlightened days of regulation: all waste, fecal and otherwise, is now carried out of the canyon.

We launched into the swirl of Kool-Aid green water that passes for the Colorado here—the silt is settled out in the reservoir 15 miles upstream and the microplankton refract their dominant hue. I gawked at a view as strange to me as another planet. Mesas, side-canyons, bosses, ramparts, benches, monoclines, faults filled an eerie landscape. We slipped between the soft red-and-maroon walls. Cliffs soared 2,000 feet on either side of our baloney boat. The din of Badger Rapid, sonorous, deep in timbre, thickened as we eased toward it.

After six months of anticipation, of poring over picture books, I was on the lip of a major Colorado rapid. Glancing to the stern where Bledsoe worked the tiller and ran the 20-horsepower outboard, I saw nonchalance unrivaled. As we slid down the coconut-butter tongue into the maw of Badger, dropping into the abyss, the crisp 47-degree water slapped me, and the pontoon pranced like a dolphin. It was over all too quickly, a matter of seconds, and we pulled over to set up camp.

We went about our tasks, erecting tables, filling buckets, clearing the shore of tamarisk. Then Bledsoe discovered that we'd forgotten the plates. His veneer of pluck seemed to crack ever so slightly as he rifled through the commissary boxes for a second look. "This is terrible," he said, his words echoing across the canyon, "How can we serve 110 geologists without plates?"

Since we were camped at the mouth of Jackass Creek, a tributary canyon, I volunteered to hike out and save the day. Bledsoe said that once I reached the road I could hitch a ride to the Hatch warehouse near Lee's Ferry, hire a jetboat capable of traveling down to the lip of Badger and back to the Ferry, and get the plates to camp by dinner. So with canteen filled, I took off alone up the side canyon in search of paper plates.

After hours of hiking, I pulled myself up onto the plateau, completely lost. I could only guess where the highway was. Kicking the red dust, passing a few prickly-pear cacti, I started east. I finally hit the road and got a ride with a Navajo in a pickup. He delivered me to the warehouse, where I picked up several cartons of paper plates, then tracked down Fred Burke, who operated the Park Service jetboat. In the waning light we surged downstream.

We got to camp just after soup, and passed out the plates in time for salad and entree. I was treated like a hero for my derring-do, and for the first time had a sense of how it felt to be a river guide.

I remember little of the next few days; I picked up an intestinal bug and spent much of the time heaving over the gunwales, other moments in delirium, collapsed on the duffel as we caromed through rapids, swept past unconformities, synclines, and other geological phenomena. At trip's end, I fully expected to be fired. In my own estimation, I had been a lousy swamper, sick for the majority of the passage, sluggish in my chores, unused to the harsh sun and physically demanding days.

But Hatch kept me on. He assigned me to the boat-patching detail at Marble Canyon Lodge, a ramshackle motel near Navajo Bridge. For a month, I lived the life of a desert rat and filled my days with barge cement and neoprene patching material under a brutal sky. Every few days another trip went out, and I stood aching at the Lee's Ferry ramp, waving as the rafts dipped into Paria Riffle just downstream.

Finally, a departing trip was short of help, and Dave Bledsoe requested me. I went into high gear, hustled at every turn, played vassal to Dave's river guide, and saw the canyon in all its glory. In turn, Dave showed me the ropes, literally, from half hitches to canyon history. His syllabus was 1.7 billion years worth of exposed geological formations.

But the lesson that made the deepest impression was the history in the making, the story of river guides. I witnessed, and was part of, an odd transmutation: ordinary people—most of them college dropouts, ski bums, ranchers' sons from the hard patches of Utah, New Mexico, and Arizona—became extraordinary people on the river, men who faced danger with chests and chins thrust out, with a smug curl of a smile under any circumstance, in any crisis. People a

Dave Edwards, member of the Colorado's fraternity of river guides, catches his breath after a run through Granite Rapid. Photo by Curt Smith.

bit soft at home turned gneiss-hard on the Colorado, resolute souls who held together when lawyers, doctors, and executives panicked. These were men who lured wives away, if only for a fortnight, with the arch of an eyebrow. They lived by their wits in a Spartan way: a pair of sun-faded shorts, a Buck knife, sleeping bag, a bottle of whiskey, and a pair of pliers.

My ascension of the Hatch ladder was hardly swift. I swamped seven trips that summer—a record, I believe—and never made river guide. Some newcomers were piloting by their third trip. I wasn't disappointed, though. I loved the river, lived for each run, and socked away my $20-a-day earnings.

I found it difficult to adjust to college after that summer. Where I had recently been in a whirlpool of activity, in one of the most sublime settings on the planet, I was now cloistered in pale library walls, lost among the milling thousands of students, books, and papers. But the Colorado never left me. Its silt seemed to course through my veins, and at every opportunity I launched into long-winded descriptions of how I'd spent my summer vacation. Having thoroughly learned a new language, I now *thought* in Grand Canyonese. I fancied myself a river man: that was my first and foremost identity. Being a student was an obligatory bore, one that left me drifting in a swamp of academia.

I longed to get back on the river. At long last, spring came, and again my flight to Page. This year I had graduated: Ted started me off with my own raft. Finally I was a river guide.

Peculiar things happened to me that summer. My tan deepened, my chest filled out, hair lightened and lustered. A heretofore unknown confidence surfaced, and I found people reacting to me in an entirely different manner. At school I was undistinguished academically, socially, and in sports. But on the river everything changed. I manned the rudder through the rapids, affecting that stern, purposeful look I'd picked up from Bledsoe; lectured eruditely about John Wesley Powell and geology; stirred dutch ovens over the campfire like an outdoor Julia Child. People looked to me for guidance, for wisdom, direction, political opinions, even for romance. That year I guided through the canyon the president of a Hollywood studio, a celebrated political journalist,

writers from *Newsweek*, the *New York Times*, and *Newsday*; Broadway actors, television stars, successful professionals of ever sort. I was in awe of them all. They were people I would never have been able to talk to, let alone socialize with, in the winter months. But here they were, apparently in awe of me, kowtowing, following my every direction, hanging on my every word. It was sobering stuff.

This social magic was happening to every other guide on the river, every backcountry, rough-necker-cowboy-Viet-Nam-vet-farmhand who somehow back-eddied into this elite club. River romances were as common and flighty as canyon wrens. At night, women slunk over to guides' sleeping bags in the darkness. Back in Chicago, where I was studying in the off-months, I couldn't get a date to save my life. But on the river, it seemed, I couldn't find an evening alone.

Most boatmen were quick to capitalize on this phenomenon. They sang off key before appreciative audiences, told bad jokes that sent laughter reverberating through the canyons, played rudimentary recorder tunes as passengers swayed revival style. And every guide took advantage of the rapids, all 160 of them. Those pieces of effervescence, white ribbons in the long emerald band, were chances to shine, to showcase mettle and stuff, to enhance the legend of dauntless river guide.

As big and impressive as the Colorado rapids appear, they are, by most measures, quite safe. Boatmen could flip, wrap, broach, jackknife, catch a crab, lose an oar, tubestand, endo, and swim, and be relatively assured of emerging intact in the quiet water below. But that was a professional secret. The script called for melodrama, and at each rapid, especially the majors

—Hance, Crystal, Horn—the boatmen would play the scene for all it was worth.

"Hold on tight. This next one's a killer!" Chills would course down passengers' spines, knuckles would whiten. The feeling, after all, could not be much different than flying in a thunderstorm and hearing the pilot advise you to assume the crash position, just in case.

"House Rock Rapid coming up. It flipped five boats last trip."

"Grapevine. That's where Sanderson hit the wall and rolled his baloney boat."

"Bedrock. Hatch once put a 27-foot rip in the floor of his raft here."

"Upset Rapid next. That's where Shorty Burton drowned in 1967 when his raft capsized and his lifejacket clipped onto a gas can."

And, of course, when the boatman and his crew—after crashing through Hell itself and staring defiantly into the pits of bottomless holes—purled into the calm water below, the passengers erupted in applause and praise, as though a divine hand had just delivered them from an eternity on the River Styx. At that dizzying instant, a boatman couldn't help but beam.

All this theater reached its denouement at Mile 179, Lava Falls, the grandest rapid of the Grand Canyon. Formed by lava flows from volcanic eruptions, it was named by John Wesley Powell upon his arrival at its lip on August 25, 1869. He was the first boatman to wax theatrical about the inelegant intrusion: "What a conflict of water and fire there must have been here!" he wrote. "Just imagine a river of molten rock running down into a river of melting snow. What a seething and boiling of the waters; what clouds of steam rolled into the heavens!"

Rimmed with black burnished rock, chopped into a mean-looking mess of crosscurrents and nasty, sharp holes, the rapid drops 37 feet in 300 yards, though it looks twice that steep, and has been clocked at 35 miles per hour. Statistics notwithstanding, Lava Falls strikes terror in the hearts of first-timers, swampers and boatmen included. It appears so angry, confused, and large, with no evident passage, that one's initial urge is to squat behind a rock. It is all quite deceptive, nonetheless; wherever a boat enters this thundering rapid, the chances are better than even it will issue upright, in fine shape, at the bottom. If a boat flips, and many, many have, passengers have the swim of their lives, but they generally bob out of it unscathed.

But it's here, on the pocked black banks, that the boatmen's ballet begins. Every move is choreographed, polished, and mentally rehearsed for best effect. The performance begins days upstream, with casual campfire mention of the coming confrontation. Then it builds to anecdotes over guacamole salad, tales of near disasters party to or witnessed. It dominates the conversation, building to a crescendo as the boats float to Vulcan's Anvil, a volcanic neck (the core of an ancient volcano) that sits midriver a mile above Lava Falls, looking, some boatmen say, like a 40-foot tombstone. From this point on, a hush descends on the rafts as they drift closer to the guttural groan of Lava.

The dance of danger begins at Lava's lip. The boats are beached, and in ritualistic fashion the guides climb to the sacred vantage, a basalt boulder about 50 feet above the cataract. Once there, weight shifts from heel to heel, fingers point, heads shake, and faces fall. This is high drama, and passengers eat it up. The reason people pay more money than for a three-star-hotel holiday to

Running Lava Falls: passengers and guide concentrate intently on the route through the Colorado's most famous drop. Photo by Curt Smith.

sleep on hard ground, eat stew mixed with sand, and go without hot running water and flush toilets is, quite simply, to get terrified in a safe, spectacular setting. Lava gives everyone his or her money's worth, and dividends.

After the scout, which can take half a day, the boatmen, somber as pallbearers, return to the boats to check riggings and remind passengers of flip procedures. Then they launch, one by one, into the foaming water. Lining up is the key to a clean run, one that loses no passengers or gear and doesn't flip. Once in the clenched fist of Lava, there is no control—the only thing you can do is hang on as it shakes its intruders like hot dice.

In the late sixties, all passengers would walk around the rapid because it was then deemed so dangerous. On my third canyon run, I was asked to man the front oars even though I could barely lift them. Dave Bledsoe sat behind me and bellowed commands over the pandemonium: "Right oar. No, left. Now both. Harder!" In the eye of this storm, I tried to follow orders, but it seemed to me I had barely executed a few inches of a right-oar pull when Bledsoe would clamor for the other. When we made the landing, amid applause and back slapping from our spectator-passengers, I turned to Dave and asked the all-important question: "How'd I do?" He pulled a bottle of champagne from his ammo box, shook it violently, and popped the cork so it arced across the river and into the white spinning skein of Lava's last wave. "You did great," he said with a wink.

It was several more trips before I learned the meaning of that wink: that no matter what one did with the oars, snapping hard strokes to every command or freezing the blades in place, the course taken would make no difference. It was all show for the clients on shore, real circus-performance material, and I learned to play it with Kabuki-like stagecraft.

The admiration all this brought created an almost schizophrenic state that was not easy to cope with or resolve. We were walking, rowing oxymorons. We all relished those moments of adulation on the river, but reality always returned with summer's end. Some turned to the slopes, some to carpentry or other crafts or service jobs; I went back to school. Still others dipped into the black book of summer clients and roamed from home to home, reliving the summer through slides, scrapbooks, and film, and wearing out welcomes. But wherever we wandered, whatever we did, it seemed mundane by comparison.

The Colorado irrevocably changed me as it does everyone; it fanned the flames of my ego, then doused the fire. Boatmen kept in touch in the off-season and compared notes. Everyone seemed to suffer the same fate and searched in vain for a winter's equivalent of the astral light that caressed us in the canyon. But no one found it, and we lived for the summer.

For some, this game of extreme highs and lows was too much. A bitterness developed. It carried over to the river, and was occasionally directed at the clients, the people who were responsible for building up these false egos. Usually after a winter or two of discontent, a boatman's attitude toward clients quick with the swoon and the compliments degenerated. Such clients became "dudes" or "peeps." Some veteran boatmen became cocky and smug. They sought fraternity among peers at the expense of the clients. Fooling a passenger while furthering the myth of boatman as epic hero was a justifiable and sometimes funny end.

Some of the kidding was innocent, such as the pumice routine: A client would awake and stumble over to the campfire where a black pot of coffee steamed.

"Coffee ready?" he'd ask.

The boatman would walk to the pot, bend over the brew, and drop into it a stone, which would promptly sink from sight.

"Nope. Too thin," the guide would declare and go back to kitchen chores. A few minutes later the passenger would inquire again, and the routine was repeated, with the same results.

A third time and the boatman would palm a piece of pumice and drop it into the coffee, where it would float: "Yup. Coffee's ready."

Another gambit was the scorpion shield. Being certain he was being watched (and he almost always was), the boatman would punch a small hole in a paper plate, then slide it up the bow line so it stood like a shield between the beach mooring and the raft, where the guide slept.

"What's that for?" some curious miss would inevitably ask.

"Scorpion shield. Keeps them off the boat. Hundreds of them on the beach, ya know. They come out at night. By the way, where're you sleeping tonight?"

One of the elaborate "pimps," as these pranks came to be called, involved eyeglasses. In a Flagstaff surplus store a boatman picked up a pair of glasses, the type with Coke-bottle-thick lenses, though his vision was 20-20. At Lee's Ferry, as the passengers boarded, he'd don the glasses, and go through the orientation as though the eyewear was normal attire. Then, just as his raft was about to drop into the first rapid, he would let out a mighty sneeze, and at the brink of the first wave, his glasses would sail into the bilge.

"Oh my God—I can't see!" he would cry and fumble with the tiller as the passengers looked back in horror.

Among that first generation of Colorado River guides—those who started in the sixties with the evolution of the job into a livelihood as well as an identity—some were better able than others to handle the conflict of dual self-images. After eight seasons as a river guide, one person left for Phoenix to become a repairman of air conditioners, the very machines that gulp power from the Glen Canyon Dam. Another who started with me died when he drove his sports car off a cliff after an off-season party. A third, a Vernal, Utah, boy who became a king of the river, was fired after a series of passenger abuses. He became a truck driver, then fatally shot himself.

But others became writers, photographers, doctors, lawyers, stockbrokers, politicians. And others still run the river and wear the proud badge of river guide, perhaps a bit faded now from the harsh sun.

One common current links all those who became Colorado River guides—the indelible memory of those life-asserting moments when all the universe was reduced to a cool, wrapping white wave, and with the pull of an oar or the twist of a tiller, the wave was crested and for a magical instant all was good and great.

No river guide, in fact no river runner, can escape that memory, and like some ineffable vision it beckons and cries to be repeated again and again. And every Grand Canyon guide, no matter how far his pursuits have carried him, comes back to the Colorado.

POLIO CREEK

Written and illustrated by William Nealy

Us kids called it Polio Creek, as in: "You better stay out of that ditch or you'll get polio." It drained the eastern slopes of Red Mountain, the southernmost extent of the Appalachian foothills in Alabama's central piedmont. It ran through my backyard in Homewood, one of Birmingham's many bedroom communities. Before World War I Polio Creek had been a meandering brook with gentle curves and gentler gradient. By 1950 it had been engineered, channelized, and civilized, walled on both banks eight feet high, first with sandstone, later with concrete.

Polio Creek was a crack in suburbia, a kid Ho Chi Minh Trail, the forbidden zone. Within its sheer cool walls a youngster could walk for miles without once falling under an adult's reptilian gaze. Here and there were tunnels connecting other neighborhoods to the creek, tunnels big enough to walk upright in and, on occasion, big enough to run like hell in when being pursued by adults or worse, teenagers. Naturally we were forbidden to play in the creek by the mom and dad units. "Typhoid!" "Rats!" "Snakes!" and,

obviously, "Polio!" Practically the worst thing that could happen to one of us would be to slip and fall into Polio Creek. It was a long sad walk home, dripping with the incontrovertible evidence of a sure whipping offense. Despite the hazards, I lived in Polio Creek.

Once or twice a year a flash flood would pump Polio Creek up eight or ten feet, turning it into a watery freight train whipping through Homewood faster than you could pedal a bike, light speed to a kid. We would be herded into the houses and our parents would stand looking out kitchen windows at the astonishing sight, smoking cigarettes and silently praying the furnace didn't get flooded. To the grown-ups the creek had become a limbless Godzilla, a hell snake unleashed on Homewood, slithering between the houses, hissing and throbbing. Sometimes a section of the retaining wall would get peeled off by the force of the current and entire backyards would be lost, scoured down to the old streambed. Dolls, basketballs, tires, jugs, paint cans, lumber, lawn furniture, shrubs and other suburban flotsam would begin the long journey south to the Gulf of Mexico on the crest of the flood. For years I had been contemplating just such a journey for myself.

I had a boat: a one-kid plastic rowboat-looking affair from K-Mart that also served as a wading pool, turtle pond or sled, as circumstances dictated. Conditions had to be just right to run Polio Creek: daylight, mild weather, sufficient water and absence of adult supervision. One blustery spring day in 1965 everything came together. It had rained all day and from my sixth-grade classroom I could see parents arriving early to pick

up their children, headlights on in the afternoon darkness—a good omen.

My friend Tommy and I rode our bikes home in the rain. Rainwater was gushing out of storm drains, and when we got to the bridge we saw that Polio Creek was high and going higher. We made a plan; I would float the creek and Tommy would stay ahead of me on his Schwinn Typhoon, checking my progress at each successive bridge. Since this was merely a run-through and not the actual Gulf of Mexico expedition, equipment and supplies were kept at a minimum. A boat, a paddle, and a paddler. I was only going a few blocks.

With Tommy stationed at the first bridge on my home street, I carried my boat upstream through backyards to where a smaller creek fed into Polio Creek through a break in the wall. Moving in a brisk but stealthy manner (a kid carrying a boat anywhere near a flooded creek was fair game for any nosey grown-up), I got into position on the feeder creek and slid down, out of sight. I got in the boat and paddled up to the break in the wall. Polio Creek shot past the breach with a low sucking moan, and as I cleared the wall I was snatched downstream. This was like some

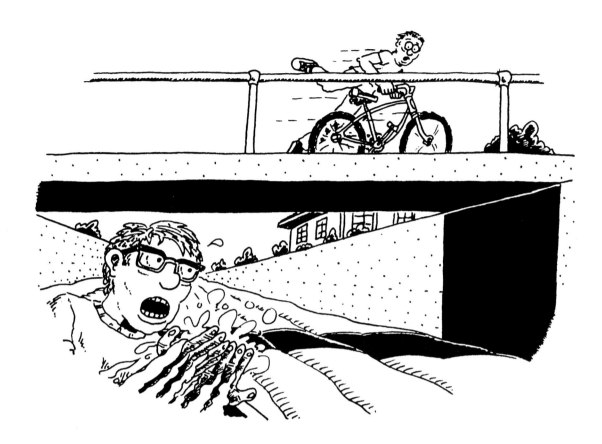

demented new ride at the state fair—a Mad Mouse with no brakes and no end, an insane machine. I was falling down a shaft with walls of concrete, water and air.

The first rapid was a 90-degree bend to the right with a huge sewage tank protruding from the left wall at the middle of the bend. The entire flow was slamming straight into the tank and folding over itself in its rush to turn right. Despite a frantic stroke or two I was heading straight into a wall of very angry-looking water. Something grabbed the boat, stood it practically on end and shoved me right at the instant before I hit the tank. Then I was bailing with my hands; water had surged over the transom into the boat as I

was tossed to the right. A huge shadow flew over me and someone yelled my name. I looked up toward the sound and saw I had just streaked under the first bridge. I could see Tommy pony-express mounting his Typhoon, heading for bridge number two.

Next bend, 90 degrees left, trying to stay to the inside of the turn. Into the wall instead, nearly vertical, then whipped left just before impact. Bailing frantically now, like those cartoons where Sylvester the cat suddenly has 50 arms. . . . My predicament is dawning on me. First it is a trickle, then a torrent of realization: I am going to drown today. Probably in the next few minutes. The walls are smooth, unbroken. Unless I can somehow stand up in the boat, I can't reach the top of the wall. The water's too deep to stand in and too fast to tread. Ninety-degree bend to the right, stayed inside the turn and only shipped a little water this time. Long curve to the left. The creek is still rising . . . I can see windows, back porches now. Great. If I don't drown I'm going to get caught. Bridge number two is coming up to meet me . . . it's like sitting in a bathtub of cold water and having the world roll over me. Tommy rides onto the bridge, drops his bike and runs to the upstream rail. He's crying now. The bridge has a center piling with a tree and some boards stuck to it. The right side would be better because there's a curve to the right just below and that would put me inside the curve. I take the left side, which looks safer, and I'm into the curve before Tommy can run to the other side of the bridge. Boat spinning, I hit the wall this time and I'm full of water. Got to bail.

Third bridge, no sign of Tommy. Water still rising and it will be a squeeze to make it under this bridge . . . less than two feet. For one second I consider grabbing the bridge and climbing up on it. Then I'm scrunched into the bottom of the

boat, flying into the penumbra of the bridge. I'm clear, on a long straightaway; ahead is bridge number four. Just below this bridge is a steel waterpipe about a foot in diameter that crosses the creek about six feet above the creek bed. I've fished from it. Now it is right at the surface, splitting the flow horizontally like a planer. A huge boil just below where the flows reunite throws steam and froth into the air. It is the end of the world. I remember a concrete storm drainpipe on the right wall just above the bridge. That is how we climb in and out of the creek here when the creek is running a trickle. It's about halfway up the wall. Right now only the top of the pipe is visible, a six-inch ledge curving into brown water. I've got to grab the pipe, roll out of the boat and climb out. There is silence and I'm looking down a dark tunnel at the top edge of a pipe and the black underside of the bridge. Nothing else exists but that little piece of concrete. I'm there . . . drop paddle . . . grab pipe . . . roll out of the boat. I swing below the pipe, planing on the surface, water tearing at my jeans. Lost a shoe, then the other. I hear a crunch as the boat is bisected by the pipe. I can't bring myself to look downstream.

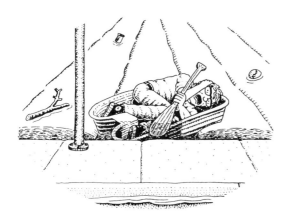

I get a leg in the pipe, then a foot on top and a hand on top of the wall. I bring my head up slowly . . . no fire trucks . . . no Tommy. The coast is clear. I cross to the far side of the bridge. Boat gone. Just brown boiling water. I hope Tommy shows up soon . . . we've got to prepare a good story in case we're interrogated later on tonight. Went wading, slipped and lost shoes. Some other kids swiped boat and sent it down creek, etc.

I see my mom's VW headed toward me, coming fast. There's my mom . . . there's Tommy. Holy crap.

ONE-WAY TRIP ON THE CLARK'S FORK

By Yvon Chouinard

Back in the mid-seventies, while I was into surfing and ice-climbing, some of of my old climbing friends got into kayaking. Being adrenalin junkies, Class V water provided them with plenty of risk to support their habits. But, not wishing to forsake their climbing roots or their need for wilderness adventure, they adapted the sport to suit their own needs. From 1980 to 1985 two of them, Royal Robbins and Doug Tompkins, along with Reg Lake and a few others, pulled off first descents of three major western Sierra rivers, the Kings, the Kern, and the San Joaquin. What was notable was that they humped their boats over 13,000-foot passes on the *east* side in order to put in at the headwaters. Big-wall climbing philosophy was applied with absolute commitment to the no-turn-back rock gorges. Even the equipment of rock climbing was used to belay blind corners and rappel unrunnable waterfalls. Being a latter-day boater, I missed out on this era and now I'm trying to play catch-up. So when I heard about an unrun river gorge near Yellowstone National Park I was definitely interested.

The Clark's Fork of the Yellowstone River comes out of the Beartooth Range near Cooke City, Montana. It drops down a sheer-walled granite canyon at the rate of 2,000 feet in 25 miles. As near as we could tell, no one had ever been all the way through the inner recesses of the gorge. Chief Joseph probably followed the ledge systems on the canyon walls to escape the Feds, who thought they had him and 800 of his people trapped in the Lamar Valley in Yellowstone in 1877. I've also heard rumors of some Montana ice climbers who have gone a ways up the gorge in winter from the bottom, using crampons and ice axes. Some fellows tried to kayak it in 1976 but after 33 portages and three days with starvation rations and beat-up boats, they left their kayaks and climbed 1,500 feet out of the canyon.

In the summer of 1984, five friends and I were ready to try it.

The team:

Yvon Chouinard, an aging surfer/climber who's always willing to be irresponsible to further a good adventure. He likes to think of himself as Badger.

Reg Lake, who owns a paddling shop near San Francisco and practices what he preaches. A veteran of the steep and deep.

Rob Lesser, a whitewater paddler/photographer who has explored the world in a kayak. Somehow each new river expedition is a piece of the Big Puzzle.

Doug Tompkins, a fashion-maker. He's been around the world more times than you've been to McDonald's. Always first to take the risks, but deadly practical.

John Wasson: A known sucker for terra incognita. The only one with a girlfriend who wishes she had come along.

The gear:

Personal gear: plastic kayak, fiberglass paddle, 1-inch webbing runner, spray skirt, sponge, helmet, lifejacket, pile paddling sweater, farmer john wetsuit, paddling jacket, baggie shorts, reef walkers or old running shoes, midweight underwear, quarter-inch-thick foam pad, 2-pound (total weight) down sleeping bag, waterproof sleeping bag cover or tarp, plastic spoon and cup, camera and film, toothbrush, aspirin, adhesive tape, waterproof stuff sacks.

Group gear: one throw rope, 120-foot 8mm rope, 120-foot 5mm rope, 5 carabiners, 15-foot tubular webbing, Swiss army knife, two breakdown paddles, matches, one cook pot, aluminum foil, one flyrod and flies.

Food for three days: muesli, powdered milk, tea and hot chocolate, cheese and crackers, sardines and oysters, salami, dried fruit, chocolate-covered espresso coffee beans, rice and pasta, dehydrated vegetable soup.

As we leave the house in Moose, Wyoming, my wife says if we aren't back in four days she is going to chicken-wire the end of the canyon and

see what comes out. Doug and Reg meet up with us in Cody, where they have been trying for two days to fly over the river for a look-see, but the weather's been awful. We want low water; that's why we're here in mid-August. Because of the rain, Rob thinks the river has come up to an "interesting" level. The shuttle, like all shuttles, is intricate. When is someone going to come up with a computer program for shuttles?

We arrive at the put-in, where the Sunlight Basin Road crosses the river, and who should show up but Kay Swanson from Billings, who was on the first kayak attempt of the Clark's Fork. He and some friends just happened to be driving by after having done a lower section of the river. This unbelievable coincidence reminds me of the early days of American climbing when, if you saw a cleated footprint on the trail, it was that of a climber, and if you caught up with him, it was a friend or a friend of a friend. There are a lot of people boating these days, but still damn few willing to accept the risks of going beyond Class III or IV. We ask Swanson for information, but he is a classic understater in the art of gamesmanship, so the only useful nugget we get is that they did not have climbing gear on their attempt.

Next to drive by is the local redneck sheriff with his C.B., bill cap, and cowboy boots. He is so fat we can't understand how he crammed himself into his little Bronco. "You boys aren't planning on going down that river are you? We had to pull the last guys out with ropes." Swanson jumps up and says that's bullshit—they didn't have any help from anybody. This is all too much for our sixth teammate, Paul Driscoll from Jackson. He decides that the Clark's Fork on this day in these conditions is just not for him and hitchhikes back to Jackson.

We finally put in at three in the afternoon and head downriver. Right away the boating is unbelievably enjoyable Class III and easy IV. Very technical, but not hard. We run everything except one long portage before making camp at 7:30. We did pass two bait fishermen armed like Mexican banditos with .357's, bandoliers across the chest and, of course, billed caps, camouflage clothes, and their redneck cooler. Now that no one backpacks anymore all you ever see in the wilderness are madmen and survivalists. We later joked about how these two guys looked like the two mountain men, the Nichols, wanted for murder in Big Sky, Montana. (The FBI later talked to each of us, wondering the same thing.)

The next day started out with four miles of flatwater through a valley reminiscent of the Merced through Yosemite. After passing a ranch-

er's cable ford, the river enters The Box, and from here on you need better eyes that I have to count the contour lines on the map. It's difficult to remember the Clark's Fork with much sense of chronology because of the constant interplay of rapids and scouting, waterfalls and portaging. The scenery was fantastic but there really was no need to remember and register the passing rapids and canyon, for turning back was not an option. We were committed to a one-way trip.

In the three days we experienced technical boating as enjoyable as it gets. Except for two long and arduous portages, most of the carries were short and easy. However, there were two places where we had to use the ropes. Once we had to ferry the boats horizontally across a cliff

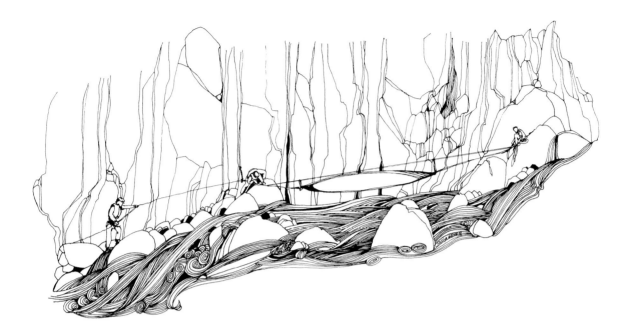

and do a little 5.7 climbing; and another time, to avoid a waterfall, we traversed a ledge and rappelled in our boats down to a pool below. Each person was lowered end-first in his boat, and the last man let himself down and pulled the double rope through. Great fun actually! Reg compared the canyon to being in the Remarkables in New Zealand and Doug thought it was like the San Joaquin. I thought of all the great climbs you could do on this beautiful granite. The approach would be easy by foot to the canyon rim, and then you could scramble down a gully to the river. I'd guess in all we ran 200 rapids, portaged 20 times,

ate plenty of rainbow/cutthroat hybrid trout, and thoroughly enjoyed our chocolate-covered coffee beans ($10 a pound). These should be illegal.

After Dead Indian Creek comes in, the contour lines go back to 100 feet per mile and in two hours we equaled the mileage of the previous two days. We bounced through the easy Class III and IV stuff of the lower canyon and spied the truck on the dirt road that crosses the river near Wyoming Route 120. We took a "*foto di grupo*," drank a bottle of good red, ate the rest of the food, loaded up, and split. Recommended. Do it before they dam it.

CHINA BY KAYAK

By Robert Portman and Dan Reicher

In the early morning mist on the muddy banks of the Yangtze, we performed the same exercise we had gone through a hundred times in our heads. As curious Chinese fishermen watched us from wooden junks moored nearby, we carefully slid aluminum tubing together and stretched the plastic skin tightly to form our two-person kayak. After years of dreaming and hundreds of pages of proposals to the Chinese government, we were within minutes and feet of our goal: to kayak the legendary Yangtze, whose mud-brown swirling waters and deep gorges had captured our imaginations.

"Hello, hello; you must take the big boat." The only English speaker in the small town of Zhongxian was Mr. Wu, a shy, thin-faced young man who, the day before, had been pressed into service by Chinese officials as our official guide. Mr. Wu spoke calmly, though he was out of breath and trembling. "Superiors have decided that little boat cannot go down big river," he said. We were crouched over the kayak, stuffing our gear bags into the compartment behind the rear seat. Another five minutes and we would have been on the water.

"Chang Jiang too big for little boat," Mr. Wu continued in his halting English. His personal concern for our safety on the Chang Jiang, the Chinese name for the Yangtze, had surfaced the previous evening. Now it had an official tone.

We had arrived in Zhongxian by water from Chongquing the day before, rare Western tourists in this crowded little river town that clings to the steep banks of the Yangtze. Leaving the ferry, we

Villagers and expedition kayak, Zhongxian, Yangtze River. Photo by Dan W. Reicher.

were immediately surrounded by a crowd of curious townspeople whose drab cotton pants and Mao-style jackets contrasted sharply with our bright nylon shorts and t-shirts. With our already dog-eared Chinese-English phrase book in hand, we attempted to ask for directions to a hotel. Our rudimentary Chinese was met with solemn stares and soft murmurings from the townspeople, some of whom were probably seeing their first Westerners. After a few uncomfortable moments, a brave school-aged girl stepped forward and muttered ''hello'' with a slight bow of her head. Laughter rippled through the crowd. Wide smiles replaced frowns and hand motions helped overcome the language barrier. A young man picked up one of our large duffel bags and led us up a steep stone stairway to the center of town.

Our entourage, gathered in front of Zhongxian's sole hotel, quickly attracted the local police. Their white jackets with brass buttons and red epaulets gave them the look of a royal greeting party. Although they seemed confused about what to do with us and concerned with the growing crowd, they were exceedingly polite. We finally followed the officers to the local police station.

After the customary cup of tea, our travel permits were checked and our self-appointed hosts set about to find a translator. This is where the hapless Mr. Wu came into the picture. A resident of a nearby town, he happened to be passing through Zhongxian that day to have his transistor radio repaired. Because he was a recent graduate of the provincial tourist school and spoke English quite well, he was drafted as our guide and keeper.

After accompanying us on a walking tour of Zhongxian, Mr. Wu joined us in our dimly lit hotel room. There he caught sight of our two oversized duffel bags, too much luggage even for Western tourists to be carrying. He glanced at the bags, then at us, too polite to ask about their contents.

Because we lacked official permission to kayak, we had kept the contents of our bags a secret while traveling overland from Beijing to the Yangtze. The only time we had been questioned about them was at customs upon our arrival in Beijing. Fearing that the aluminum poles and plastic skin might be mistaken for something more threatening, we volunteered to the customs agent that the bulky bags contained a small boat. From his blank stare we could tell that the word ''boat'' meant nothing to him. We quickly showed him a photograph of the two of us paddling a similar kayak off the coast of Maine near Acadia National Park. The agent laughed incredulously and waved us through without even a brief inspection.

Still afraid that Chinese officials might thwart our unconventional travel plans, we were reluctant to tell Mr. Wu what was in the bags. But he persisted with his questioning eyes and even reached under a bed to touch one of the bags. Out of a combination of respect for our host and interest in his reaction, we explained that we had a small boat which we planned to paddle down the Yangtze.

Mr. Wu laughed a bit nervously at what he must have thought was a joke. However, when we pulled a collapsible wooden paddle from one of the bags, his disbelief turned to concern for our safety: ''No, no, Chang Jiang too big for little boat. Come with me tomorrow morning. We can go by big boat to next town. Much better.''

As we looked up at a nervous Mr. Wu the next morning by the river, we were determined not to go on the ''big boat.'' We rose to our feet to convince our host that the Yangtze, for all its legendary might, would present no danger to us in the small boat we had assembled on the riverbank. Drawing a map of the United States in the wet sand with a river reed, we traced major rivers we had navigated in our kayaks: the Colorado, the Rio Grande, the Ohio, the Hudson. . . .

Our recital of mighty American rivers was lost on Mr. Wu. "The big boat leaves soon—in one hour," he explained. But we would not back down. After 15 minutes of polite but tense negotiations, Mr. Wu finally agreed we could make our case to a higher authority, the chief of police of Zhongxian.

The chief, a frail little man in a starched white coat, was summoned to the riverbank to watch us demonstrate our kayaking skills. By now, a couple of hundred townspeople had gathered on the bank and several dozen more watched from fishing boats and barges in the harbor. As we shook hands with the police chief he glanced nervously at our tiny boat, then at the burgeoning crowd. He seemed a reluctant judge.

Despite what we had told Mr. Wu about paddling the great rivers of America, we had never had the chance to paddle this particular kayak anywhere. Three young boys, dressed in faded shorts and plastic sandals, waded into the river to give us a push. Our first strokes were tentative but, coaching each other, we began to paddle more smoothly. We maneuvered the kayak between the fishing boats moored along the riverbank. A rusty cable separated the harbor from the main channel of the river. From our seats we grabbed the cable and pulled the boat across, bloodying our hands in the process.

The power of the river surprised us, tipping the kayak on its side. We paddled hard, managing to right the boat and never breaking our smiles in the process. We practiced our ferrying in the current for a few minutes and then returned to the calm harbor where our audience and the pacing police chief waited.

Nodding heads and smiling faces told us that the townspeople approved of our maiden voyage. We were pleased as well, for in those few minutes on the Yangtze we had probably become the first Westerners to kayak in China. Unfortunately, the excitement of the moment was lost on the man whose views counted most. After conferring with the grim-faced chief of police, who by now had been joined by five or six lieutenants, Mr. Wu announced that we would have to accompany him downstream on the "big boat." With one last look toward the now expressionless crowd, we relented. Forcing a smile, the chief ordered his officers to assist us in dismantling the kayak. We shook hands and thanked him in our phrase-book Chinese. Although discouraged, we knew that there would be other opportunities to test the swift waters of the Yangtze.

After treating us to a meal of rice and an unidentifiable but delicious fried meat, Mr. Wu accompanied us downriver on a small ferry boat which we shared with chickens and pigs. We passed the time on the noisy and malodorous deck playing Chinese checkers with Mr. Wu on his board imported from the United States. He won every game. At dusk, we arrived in Sibaozhai, a farming community named for the ancient pagoda that towers above it.

Despite our setback, we remained determined to kayak the Yangtze. The trip had been in the planning stages for over five years, since our graduation from Dartmouth College in 1979. In 1977,

Villagers unloading boats, Sibaozhai, Yangtze River. Photo by Dan W. Reicher.

we were part of the first expedition on record to navigate the entire length of the 1,888-mile Rio Grande. Two years later we were ready for a new kayak adventure. Unfortunately, in 1979 China was not ready for us. Foreign tourists were just beginning to travel in the country and only then on tightly controlled tours. The best one could hope for was an expensive package tour that might include a couple of days on the Yangtze on a luxury cruise ship. By 1982, however, China, as part of a rapprochement with the West, had opened its doors to independent travelers.

With China's new approach toward tourism, we thought the time was ripe to test the Yangtze's waters by kayak. However, after two years and sev-

eral proposals to the Chinese government, we were unable to obtain the official permission we had hoped for. At the same time, we were never told we couldn't undertake the voyage. Following our graduation from law school, we decided to take our chances. We flew to China in August of 1984 with our 50-pound collapsible kayak.

After reaching Sibaozhai, Mr. Wu settled us into a comfortable room on the grounds of the majestic pagoda, an eight-story temple built about 1200 A.D. The pagoda is not equipped for tourists, but Mr. Wu and the other guides set up a room for us in their quarters. After the morning's incident on the riverbank, the high walls and locking gate of the ancient structure must have reassured them that we would still be around the next morning with the "little boat" packed safely away.

After dinner, our Chinese hosts arranged a basketball game on the local dirt court. Undoubtedly, they assumed that all young Americans were skilled practitioners of the sport. So did the 300 or so residents of the town who ringed the court and crowded nearby balconies to watch us play. They all soon learned, however, that we had spent more of our youth in kayaks than on basketball courts. Fortunately, we had learned some of the flourishes—if not the mechanics—of the game. Our through-the-leg dribbling, "high fives," and behind-the-back passes didn't earn us many points, but the howls of laughter from the crowd made us feel like the Harlem Globetrotters. We lost by a wide margin, but our team received a standing ovation anyway. In Chinese style, we applauded ourselves as well as the victorious team.

The following day we said goodbye to Mr. Wu, who seemed genuinely sorry to see us go. The next stop on the local ferry boat was Wanxian. Sadly, Wanxian, like Zhongxian and Sibaozhai before it, would not see the stern of our kayak. Searching the riverfront one evening for a suitable launching point, we were greeted in French by a tall Chinese man sporting a Western-style jacket. "*Bonsoir. Vous êtes les jeunes Américains avec le petit bateau?*" Shocked that he knew about us and our kayak, we replied in what remained of our college French that we had arrived in Wanxian aboard the "big boat."

News of our exploits seemed to have traveled as swiftly as the Yangtze. When our French-speaking friend explained that he was the regional minister of tourism, we knew it was more than a coincidence that we had met him on the dark

riverbank that evening. The next morning we dejectedly boarded a local steamer bound for yet another small river town, Yuyang. Because only one city downstream of Yuyang remained on our travel permit, we knew that the following day we would have our last opportunity to paddle the Yangtze.

Reaching Yuyang just before nightfall, we checked into a hotel and carefully packed our provisions for what we hoped would be a full day's journey on the river. We rested but could not sleep as the anticipation built. Taking no chances this time, we arose at 3:30 A.M., before even the early-rising Chinese began to stir. A nearly full moon lighted the rocky path down to the river. We assembled the boat in record time, spurred on by the mumblings in an adjacent houseboat, which we knew would soon produce curious onlookers.

Still adjusting our spray cover and lifejackets, we pushed off into the dark, swirling waters, uncertain of what we would find. No sooner had we started, though, than we were hit by a barrage of searchlights and the growl of a noisy engine that seemed to be coming from the riverbank. We retreated to the opposite side in an attempt to escape the blinding lights. A voice boomed out over a loudspeaker. Never before had we wished so much that we could understand Chinese. However, from the speaker's authoritarian tone we got the distinct impression that our voyage, all 15 minutes of it, was about to end.

Then, suddenly, the searchlight dimmed and the roar of the engine grew fainter. An enormous barge worked its way past us upstream without stopping. After battling the barge's wake, we paddled hard to get as far as possible downriver before sunrise.

The Yangtze is an awesome river, especially

when experienced from a kayak. It is more than 3,000 miles long and flows at great speed—in places more than 20 m.p.h.—and reaches depths of many hundreds of feet. Huge whirlpools erupt out of nowhere. Avoiding them proved a challenge; thankfully, most of those that caught us were more innocent than they looked. Some river travelers were not so fortunate. Midmorning we came upon a man in a whirlpool—face down and bloated.

Paddling proved especially challenging when, after several hours, we came to Qutang Gorge, the first of the Three Great Gorges of the Yangtze that stretch for 120 miles between Chongquing and Yichang. Qutang's sheer rock walls compress the Yangtze to half its width, increasing the river's turbulence and head winds. Until 1959, when the Chinese began a massive project to rid the gorges of reefs and shoals, navigation was treacherous for even the most skilled boatmen. In a kayak the going was still rough, but our efforts were more than made up for by the magnificent gorge that rose around us.

Sadly, we were to learn a few days later that Qutang's beauty, as well as that of the Wu and Xiling gorges below it, may not outlast this century. The Three Gorges hydroelectric dam, which will be the largest in the world when completed, is expected to flood all three. The Bureau of Reclamation of the United States Department of the Interior is assisting China in the construction of this massive project. The joint effort has been hailed as an important landmark in U.S.-China relations. We weren't so sure.

Closer on the horizon, the Gezhouba dam project, downriver of the Three Gorges, will slow the Yangtze's speed and raise the river's level, forcing over one million people to relocate. We felt fortunate to have tested the Yangtze's waters before

they are fully tamed. We also pondered the apparent absence of opposition to the massive dams. Not only were no "Save the Gorges" t-shirts or citizens' petitions to be found, but local Chinese who were aware of the projects voiced no dissent.

Once through Qutang Gorge, we were able to relax and enjoy the beauty around us. The intricately layered landscape that we floated past spoke of many centuries of human habitation. The rocky riverbanks gave way to terraces of green where rice paddies were tended by stooped farmers and water buffalo pulling plows. Always there was someone watching us, undoubtedly wondering about our strange craft. Children tending goats high up in the craggy banks waved to us and women washing by the riverside looked up from their work. Foot travelers also followed our progress as they traversed rocky paths originally built so men and women in harness could pull boats upstream.

Not far from our destination, the bustling river town of Wushan, the luxury cruise ship *Three Gorges* passed us. American tourists on the deck spied us and the U.S. flags we had hoisted at either end of our small craft. They gave us a rousing cheer. After much waving back and forth and a deep blast from the ship's horn, they passed us bound for Shanghai. A touch of patriotism gave us renewed energy for our last few miles of paddling. After one hundred exhausting and at times treacherous miles we were happy to arrive in Wushan. From there we boarded a larger boat and spent three lazy days watching the river from a safer and drier vantage point and reflecting on the adventure we had just had.

The past five days had been every bit as much a political challenge as an athletic one. Rob, with his gracious manner and State Department experience, had assumed the role of the expedition diplomat, calming Mr. Wu that first morning on the riverbank and assuring that we would not leave Zhongxian on the "big boat" without an appeal to the chief of police. Dan, a wiry, curly-haired fellow with 12 years of river-running experience, made sure that if we were detained in China it would not be by one of the Yangtze's whirlpools. In all of this we drew on our experience together on the Rio Grande 7 years earlier. The six-month expedition had almost collapsed as a result of personality conflicts and a struggle over leadership. The experience taught us that it is the spirit of compromise more than anything else that insures that friendships are not lost in the often turbulent waters of an expedition.

Following a two-day stopover in Shanghai, China's largest and most cosmopolitan city, we headed south for more kayaking. Our destination was West Lake, which has long been a favorite vacation spot for Chinese and foreigners alike. Formal gardens ring the large man-made lake, which was constructed by hand beginning in 821 A.D. Islands, studded with formal tea gardens and intricate paths, dot its surface. For nearly 1,000 years, the lake and adjacent city of Hangzhou served as a residence and playground for a succession of Song and Qing dynasty emperors and their guests. Legend has it that Marco Polo stopped here on his epic Asian voyage.

We were intrigued by the prospect of kayaking among the islands and gardens of this enchanted lake. Following our successful practice on the Yangtze, we arose early, slipping our craft into the lake's smooth waters before daybreak. We paddled in silent rhythm, breathing in the sweet, flower-scented air.

We thought we were dreaming when we first sighted kayaks on the horizon. But the low-slung boats and rapidly moving paddles were unmistakable. In all of our research we had uncovered no evidence that the sport of kayaking existed in China. In fact, the All China Sports Federation—the official Chinese sports agency—had answered our proposals to kayak by politely assuring us that the sport was unknown in China. Yet there they were, six needle-sharp flatwater-racing kayaks, skimming across West Lake's silken waters.

When the six muscular kayakers—three men and three women—spotted us, they pointed toward our boat and talked excitedly. Next to their sleek fiberglass boats with foot-controlled rudders, our bulbous and by now dirty soft-skinned kayak was unimpressive. But this did not deter our friends, after a quick greeting, from taking our ungainly craft for a spin.

Unfortunately, the Chinese kayakers' English was nearly as deficient as our Chinese. However, through a combination of drawings, hand signals and help from our phrase book we were able to trade our respective stories. We learned that they were members of a national flatwater kayak team with designs on the 1988 Olympics. When we told them about our adventure on the Yangtze, they were as incredulous as Mr. Wu had been. But they nodded approvingly when we told them our next and final stop was the Li River, famed throughout China for its unique beauty.

The language we had most in common was kayaking. We spent the day exchanging paddling techniques and trading boats, sometimes forming a joint Chinese-American team in our kayak. At the end of the day we presented our friends with an American flag from our boat and prom-

Boatman at dusk on the Li River near Guilin, Guangxi Province. Photo by Dan W. Reicher.

ised to meet again sometime on the water. The prospect of kayaking the Li made saying goodbye a little bit easier.

Our first view of the Li came at sunset from a mountaintop near the city of Guilin. The fatigue from a 36-hour train ride disappeared as we caught sight of the river. The Li wends its way through a landscape perhaps unrivaled in the world. Sheer-walled limestone towers jut skyward from an undulating green plain dotted with rice paddies. Of this enchanted land the celebrated Tang dynasty poet Han Yu wrote in the eighth century: "The river forms a green silk belt, the mountains are like blue jade hairpins."

The city of Guilin, bound to the east by the Li River, sits at the edge of this magical landscape. As a result of its location, Guilin has felt the impact of the recent increase in tourism like no other city in China. All over town, entrepreneurs with a newfound capitalistic fervor hawk Li River t-shirts, panda mugs, and Great Wall rugs to tourists sporting Mao hats. In the shadows, young men whispering "change money?" lure tourists into trading their Foreign Exchange Certificates (the official tourist currency) for greater quantities of "People's Money." Chinese who succeed in this black-market exchange buy scarce foreign goods with the Foreign Exchange Certificates.

**Li River and limestone peaks near Guilin,
Guangxi Province. Photo by Dan W. Reicher.**

We didn't linger long in Guilin, preferring instead the less-crowded countryside. Almost by habit now, we arose hours before the sun to begin our journey. We assembled the boat amidst tall grass at the river's edge. We worked quickly and were soon paddling away from the city under a dark sky.

The Li flows in stark contrast to the mighty Yangtze. The river is barely a stone's throw in width and but a few feet deep. Its transparent green waters move almost imperceptibly. The slow current and clear water make for ideal swimming, and not only for humans. Just downstream from Guilin we came upon a herd of water buffalo up to their haunches in the water and munching lazily on river grass. Fortunately, the massive, broad-horned beasts seemed to have no interest in us, even as we back-paddled nervously to avoid them.

Boats of all types ply the Li's waters. Most abundant are the narrow bamboo rafts, which are poled through the water. At the center of the raft often sits a basket containing a large dark bird, the famed fishing cormorant. A coil of rope is attached to a brass ring around the bird's neck. The fisherman sets the bird gently upon the water and holds tight to the other end of the rope. Almost instantly, the cormorant dives toward the bottom, sometimes surfacing with a fish too large to pass the brass ring around its neck. The fisherman plucks the fish from the bird's beak, places it in the basket, and sets the bird back on the water again. We never grew tired of watching this wonderful collaboration between man and animal.

By midafternoon, after many hours in the hot sun, we were tired and running low on drinking water. Our parched mouths brought back memo-

**Boatman with cormorant basket on Li River near
Guilin, Guangxi Province. Photo by Dan W. Reicher.**

ries of the Rio Grande. At a widening in the river we finally came upon the little town of Xinping. We left our boat at the river's edge and walked up a steep bank toward a newly built structure that appeared to be a hotel. In the dark and cool hotel we found much-needed drinking water and a room for the night.

Returning to the river to retrieve our boat and luggage we found two young Chinese boys paddling our kayak in circles in the middle of the river. We waved our arms frantically urging them to shore. The boys appeared confused by our angry response. Their reaction seemed to reflect a communal view of property now familiar to us after six weeks in China. On our long train rides, for example, our packs would be opened and English-language books, family photographs, and even our cameras would be passed around an entire train car. Our belongings were always

returned to us in perfect order just as, in time, the kayak was delivered to shore. Just the same, we gladly accepted the hotel manager's offer to store our muddy boat in the lobby.

We began our final day on the Li paddling into a soft mist lit by the glow of dawn. As the mist dispersed, the morning sun highlighted the lush mountains spread before us. At midmorning a string of brightly festooned tour boats cruised past. Tourists, mostly Chinese, crowded the railings and cheered us on as we tried to keep pace with the fast-moving boats.

By afternoon the spectacular mountains gave way to the more typical Chinese countryside: a patchwork of rice paddies, small plots of vegetables and clusters of low, tile-roofed buildings. Rounding the bend, we saw the little town of Yangsuo where we would end our trip on the Li. Drifting toward town, where passengers were leaving the tour boats, we reflected on our journey through China. Our early-morning disappointment on the banks of the Yangtze had been replaced by a flood of warm and enduring memories. At the same time, we were saddened that the magnificent Yangtze gorges might one day be flooded by the new dams. We wondered as well how many more visitors the Li can absorb without losing its magical aura; and how modernization and an opening to the West would change the people of China, whose patience and hospitality had made our journey with the "little boat" so special.

DEEP TROUBLE

By Peter N. Skinner

The Lewiston, New York, cop, who could have been half my age, motioned with his finger for me to come over and have a word with him. "You're in trouble—deep!" was all he said and he didn't get out of the squad car. My fellow paddler, Bob Patraw, terrified all over again, whispered in my ear, "Will we be fined, huh?" Now what kind of question was that after surviving the Niagara Gorge in a kayak?

It was the nth time that day that I'd been in trouble, but that's the way things are on the Niagara Gorge. A mile below the falls themselves, the 500-foot-deep gorge offers 4,000 feet of spectacular rapids. They flow at 100,000 cfs and 35 miles per hour, dropping about 50 feet and ending in the mysterious and swirling Whirlpool. It is some of the biggest whitewater in North America. Vertical-faced, 20-foot-high green curling "rogue" waves collapse when their foundations are swept from beneath them by the raging current and then rise again on ten-second cycles; huge boils and whirlpools emerge out of nowhere. On shore, police lurk everywhere, then sweep in to arrest.

Enough to shake the confidence of the most intrepid paddler.

Over the centuries the Niagara Gorge has seen all kinds of kinky adventures: couples floating to their deaths on ice flows; high-wire artists swinging perilously overhead; barrel after barrel plunging like submarines through the rapids, only to spin round and round in the Whirlpool's grand eddy; and other victims too numerous to catalog.

For decades, kids used to swim across the Maid of the Mist Pool below the falls, the end of which is called the Swiftdrift, the rapidly accelerating ocean of water that gushes downward into the gorge. They dared each other to start closer to the rapids; some didn't make it across and were swept away.

One of the most notable craft to navigate this fearsome stretch successfully was the Maid of the Mist steamer herself. In 1861, Captain Joel Robinson had a tough job on his hands. He had agreed to sell the sight-seeing boat if it made it through the rapids to Lake Ontario intact.

So he and two others steamed down the Swift-

Stereo photograph of Peter Skinner on the Niagara Gorge. To see this photo in 3-D, view the left print with the left eye and the right print with the right eye, then merge a common point in each print. Photo by Joe E. Maskasky.

drift on June 6 and into 250,000 cfs of tumult. (After two downstream hydro projects were built, the flow over the falls was reduced by international agreement to 100,000 cfs during summer days.) According to one account, foam enveloped the entire craft and waves crashed onto the decks. The wheel was wrenched from the captain's hands and the first mate thrown through the bridge door and knocked unconscious. Below, the fireman clung desperately to a post and prayed. In spite of this terrifying abuse, the plucky Maid arrived in one piece and was sold into more tranquil service on Lake Ontario's placid waters.

Other craft have not always been as fortunate. In 1887, Charles Percy tried the rapids in an "unsinkable" wood-and-canvas boat with 900 pounds of ballast. Surprisingly, he survived both the waves and 25 minutes in the Whirlpool's "great eye." The next year, Robert Flack of Syracuse was killed when his similar boat was swallowed by the "black hole" of the Whirlpool and spat out vertically, landing on top of him. Undeterred by these mishaps, one Walter Camp-

bell tried the rapids a bit later in an ordinary open boat, paddling standing up, along with his dog; he swam, the dog drowned.

In 1976, George Butterfield of Toronto and Jerry Morton of Casper, Wyoming, received permission to begin commercial rafting runs of the gorge. On the 12th run, with 27 passengers aboard, a monstrous wave flipped the 35-foot-long Zodiac raft as Morton attempted to direct it from the left side of the river to the middle. Three passengers drowned and another person died later attempting to recover the empty raft as it spun round and round in the Whirlpool. Much litigation ensued.

It is not surprising then that the Niagara Falls State Park Commission tries to stop people from doing anything but sightseeing on or near the gorge. Both New York and Canada prevent launching of private boats on the Niagara River without a permit. Two fearless souls back in the early 1980s put in anyway on a sunny October Sunday on the Canadian side of the Maid of the Mist Pool. They were immediately discovered, of course, and chased by constabulary in helicopters, patrol cars, and on foot along the mile-long flatwater pool. Horns and sirens blared and loudspeakers warned the paddlers of the dire legal consequences and danger of their intended passage. Spooked by the reception, one capsized immediately, swam the entire gorge, and paid a sizable fine after rescuing himself and being apprehended. The other escaped into the woods, retrieving his kayak, unnoticed, the next day.

Every hardcore New York paddler dreams (or has nightmares) of plying these forbidden waters. After two surreptitious runs myself, the gorge remained terrifying, but, oh, so seductive. I hadn't planned to do it again for a while, but Bob Patraw, a paddler with a bombproof Eskimo roll, kept bugging me about trying. I was eventually convinced. In the fall of 1985 we headed down the New York State Thruway to sneak our boats once more down the bank into the gorge at midnight. Returning the next day in jogger's togs, we dragged the boats to the river and Bob spent hours frightening himself as he scouted the immense crashing waves.

The first time I ran it, I was crazed with panic; the second time I was still terrified. This time, however, I was only frightened. But Bob . . . well, he was a basket case, though resolutely committed, come what might. I didn't let on to him that I had some reservations myself.

At midday, the river at its peak flow, we slid into our boats under cover of the riverside shrubs. The smudge of fear and foreboding was palpable. The smell and sight of gray industrial river water didn't help any, contrasting vividly with the bright yellow plastic kayaks on its surface. And it made the obligatory practice rolls mighty unpleasant. As we waited for the tourist helicop-

ter to disappear downriver for what we hoped would be a long time, Bob struggled to affix his uncooperative spray skirt. "Christ," I growled, "how many damn times have you done that before without a problem?" Desperation was indeed setting in!

As soon as we emerged discreetly from beneath the bushes along the shore, someone on the Whirlpool Rapids Bridge high above us yelled some encouragement. Then, the helicopter came back up the gorge and horns honked enthusiastically on the rim. You might say we'd been noticed.

Bob was white as a sheet as the irresistible current dragged us ever faster down the Swiftdrift toward the rogue waves. The sight of hydraulic explosions 30 feet high was horrifying. The gorge walls literally flew by and the wind whistled through my helmet.

After surmounting the introductory river-wide cross curler, I spun around to wish Bob well in the crashing froth ahead. It didn't help—he still appeared paralyzed with fear—so I spun the boat downstream. Running sideways, I hit the first wave. I stabbed it with my right blade and clung to my brace as the wave reared up beneath the boat. In a flash, however, my boat and I crested the wave, safe for now. I thought.

Rogue Wave Number I had other ideas. The speed of the water had undermined the support for the wave's crest. When I looked upstream for a moment, my heart sank, literally—20 feet of air separated me from the upstream trough. Down I fell, instantly enveloped in the guts of the Niagara. Finally, some light, then a very slow roll; now ready for more.

Reality reorientation. A glance at the deck revealed that my spray skirt was entirely off! The boat, lacking front float bags, wallowed uncontrollably, and the rest of the gorge was still ahead. What little self-assurance previous runs had generated sank without a trace along with the bow of the kayak.

But there was no time to contemplate my predicament. Rogue II loomed, poised to pounce. I remember a fleeting notion that the green face of the wave would shear me off at the midsection as my momentum drove the kayak's bow deep into it.

Caught in the guts of this underwater washing machine, twisting turbulence nearly wrenched me from the boat. Underwater for so, so long . . . Finally, some light. I tried two rolls, but the kayak refused to respond. Half out of the boat, I caught a breath, and made the third roll successfully. Just in time; Rogue III reared up to finish me off.

I was submerged again, and the wild tumbling reached a new high. I was running out of air and worried about a swim, my first in years. "How ignominious," I thought, "to swim here in my home state on a river the officials have tried to convince everyone is unrunnable. Could they have been right?" I tried more rolls, got some breath once and stubbornly settled myself back in the seat to try some more. Finally, the seventh (or tenth—I lost count) roll brought me up. That was one sweet and very deep breath!

Compared to the Rogues behind me now, the tortured boils and extraordinary eddy fence that lay between me and the shore seemed almost benign. In fact, after the abuse I had taken, paddling the disabled boat, its tail high in the air, into the eddy above the Whirlpool almost seemed like fun.

Regaining some semblance of composure, I suddenly remembered Bob was behind me somewhere. Searching the waves frantically, I finally spied him, emerging from the last big crashing wave, rolling again himself. Once upright, he screamed jubilantly, happy to be alive, spray skirt intact! I emptied my boat beneath the hovering Coast Guard helicopter and swore one more time at my lousy drumhead spray skirt. "I guess we've been caught," I ruefully observed to Patraw.

We quickly set off again, fighting the extraordinary boils and 200-foot-wide eddy line separating us from the true path to the deep vortices of the Whirlpool. After blasting through its monster guard hole, we finally relaxed, surfing the run-out waves and spinning in the boils between the giant power plants straddling the lower gorge.

Last stop, the Lewiston Dock on Lake Ontario's placid flatwater. No one was there to greet us but the bright fall sun. Big water, big fright, big success, and no arrest!

About that time, the Lewiston police car pulled into view, lights flashing. Eventually, he let us off with just a warning.

In the fall of 1987, litigation by the American Whitewater Affiliation forced the New York State Office of Parks to issue paddling permits to three parties, and more than a dozen paddlers experienced the gorge for the first time. Three low-volume squirt boats blasted through the turbulence, and Nolin Whitesell of Georgia made the run in an open canoe. He rolled once.

Media coverage of the first legal run was substantial, but not exactly laudatory. "Riding Lower Niagara Rapids Dumb Idea, Bad Example," read the headline on one editorial.

The New York parks office agreed. Because one

paddler spent an inordinate amount of time upside down just above the Whirlpool, state officials halted further paddling by barring access to the river. They said that rescue efforts would be too expensive and dismissed the AWA's offer to screen paddlers seeking permits.

But theirs may not be the last word. Paddlers are continuing the legal fight to paddle the Niagara's wild waters.

Much of the historical information contained in this chapter was drawn from *Niagara! Eternal Circus* by Gordon Donaldson (Toronto: Doubleday Canada Limited; Garden City, N.Y.: Doubleday & Co., Inc., 1979).

SANTA MARIA!

By Jamie McEwan

I am crawling along a rock ledge on the right bank of the Rio Santa Maria. The left bank, across from us, is a 280-foot cliff, and from the top of that cliff another river is falling on us.

We had heard about this place; we'd been warned by our Mexican contact that if the upper river, the Gallinas, was at a high level, its falling waters would block off the entire canyon. So we had checked the Gallinas before we started our trip on the Santa Maria, three days before. It had been low.

Then last night, without warning, five inches of rain had fallen.

The only thing I can see clearly is the bright yellow of my brother's nylon pants as he crawls along in front of me. A continuous blast of water pellets—it would be misleading to call the stuff spray—hits us from my left. There is so much water in the air that I have to breathe carefully to avoid choking. It's like trying to scout a rapid while someone blasts a fire hose into your face.

The legs before me stop, and Tom shouts something.

"I can't hear you!" I shout back.

He starts to back up, and we retreat to where the ledge is wider. Tom turns to face me, bringing his head over until our helmets touch. Even this close, he has to shout to be heard over the roar of the falls:

"The ledge ends. Maybe you could jump in the water there, swim around the point. But I don't know."

"Let me go out and look," I shout back.

Tom nods. I crawl back out along the ledge, my eyes nearly closed, until I reach forward with my hand into empty space. End of ledge.

There are momentary lulls in the wind, when it is possible to get a glimpse of my surround-

Mexico's Tamul Falls, where the Rio Gallinas tumbles 280 feet into the Rio Santa Maria, makes the Santa Maria impassable on this trip and forces a climb out of the canyon. Photo by Wick Walker.

ings. The trick is to open your eyes at the right instant. From many glimpses I piece together an image of an eddy, a pool of quieter water before me. But with rock on three sides, and the fourth side open to the force of the plummeting Gallinas, it could as easily be a trap as a haven. The rock itself is coated with travertine deposited by the limestone-rich water: no cracks, just a smooth expanse, as if it all had been stuccoed. No footholds.

With just five seconds of calm I could make a reasonable assessment of the situation. But it's hard even to think under that steady drumming. I retreat.

"If you jump in, I'm not sure where you'd climb out again," I shout to Tom. He nods, and we go back to where Andy Bridge and Wick Walker wait by the boats. For the first time since I came to Mexico I am cold.

"We can't portage around this side," I tell them.

"We'll have to go back upstream and climb around the other side," Wick says. "Let's look it over."

We launch our boats on top of the driftwood that is trapped against this shore. The force of the wind is causing waves to run upstream, against the current, and we ride them across the river to the sheltered spot from which we had first viewed the falls.

It was October 1985. From some paddling friends, we had heard about the Santa Maria (located about 100 miles north of Mexico City) and decided to run it. We had arrived at the point where the Gallinas enters the Santa Maria happy and excited from a morning of the best kind of river running. Each rapid, at first glance, had threatened to be unrunnable, but each time we

could locate eddies that offered the chance to pause midstream and find the next opening. So we would descend, hopping from pool to pool, darting through narrow slots, dropping over ledges, switching the lead, arriving at the bottom excited by each successful solution.

But the group is sober now.

Looking at the falls from here it's hard to imagine that it could be much of an obstacle. Four main spouts leave the clifftop, spreading as they fall into feathery plumes of spray that look wonderfully soft and cool. The spray boils up against the far canyon wall, rising more than the full height of the waterfall itself. A perfect backdrop for, say, an ad for beer or mentholated cigarettes. It is hard to reconcile the way it looks with the miniature hurricane we had experienced a few minutes before.

Standing on the rocky shoreline, we talk it over, sharing a ration of granola.

Andy wants to try paddling under the falls. "It might hurt, but it won't actually damage you," he concludes, smiling.

Wick says, rather mildly, that he thinks we should climb around. The mildness shows that he's not giving orders, not speaking as team leader—just offering an opinion.

I'm with Andy. "Look," I say, "one guy paddles—the rest go out on the ledge as safety. If the paddler gets pinned against the shore, we can throw him a rope, pull him out."

"All right, let's do it," Andy says, with his never-failing enthusiasm.

"We do have a harness for the swimmer," Wick says. "I don't know, though."

"Are you willing to be the paddler?" Tom asks, looking me in the eye.

"I sure am."

Andy Bridge on the Santa Maria. The river carves the limestone into strange
formations that make the paddling challenging. Photo by Wick Walker.

"I am, too," Andy says.

"Climbing around is a sure thing, though," Wick argues. "We could waste a lot of time trying to paddle by, and if it doesn't go, the climb's still going to be a lot of work."

"Well, yeah," I say. "We should sort of agree." I look over at Tom. "What do you think? I mean, only the two of us were there on that ledge."

Tom doesn't reply right away.

I am confident of the outcome. In fact, I feel a little devious, leaving it up to my brother Tom, the bravest person I know, right up to and sometimes over the line that separates brave from foolhardy. He had been up to his usual standards on this trip. Before we started I had secretly vowed to run any rapid that Tom did, but we weren't

more than a few hours into the first canyon of the Rio Santa Maria when I'd had to eat that promise.

Later that same day he'd crossed the line into the foolhardy area. I wasn't the least bit embarrassed to be manning a rescue rope while he paddled. The rapid was a double drop, the first onto some shallow rocks, and the second flowing against a vertical rock wall—tough, but runnable. But 30 yards below the second drop the entire river flowed underneath a tremendous, house-sized boulder. It simply disappeared.

There were a lot of strange formations on the Santa Maria. The rock is limestone, easily carved and shaped by the river. We had encountered one large boulder that was hollow, with two small "windows" in the side; we had seen streams that poured directly out of the vertical canyon walls. More than once, we'd seen the river flow under boulders, like this.

These were the kind of spots I didn't even like to look at for too long, because when I look at any piece of water, I start to imagine paddling it. And to watch the water flow into a crack between two rocks and then disappear into a dark hole is to imagine being sucked underground, fighting to get through a passage that would inevitably be choked by driftwood and debris. Not pleasant even to think about.

Nor was it pleasant to watch my brother hit the bow of his kayak hard on a rock at the bottom of the first drop, pop his spray skirt, slam against the wall in the second drop, almost flip, and arrive at the bottom of the rapid with a boat half full of water, struggling to reach the safety of the eddy before being swept into the terminal wall.

There was nothing we could do but shout encouragement. Shout we did. Tom ended up against the rock, only ten feet above the strainer. He poled off hard and paddled to safety.

Later Tom admitted he shouldn't have run that one.

So I left this decision—to run the river under the waterfall, or to climb out of the canyon—up to Tom. If something seemed even feasible to me, then Tommy probably would think it was a piece of cake.

To my surprise Tom votes to portage. "It's so hard to know what's happening in there," he says. "It might just be too strong for us. We have a limited amount of strength, you know. Just so much."

I'm on the verge of appealing to his sense of adventure, his curiosity, but a sudden thought holds me back. Maybe he's right. If Tommy hesitates, there might be good reason to hesitate.

"Well . . . yeah . . . O.K.," I say. "I don't want to do it unless we agree on it." I look at Andy and shrug. He nods. I feel all geared up for action, and I transfer that energy to the new problem. I shoulder my boat and start for the cliff.

Two hours later I'm at the top. Tommy is 50 feet below me, Wick and Andy and the four boats —three C-1s and Tom's kayak—are all in a cave somewhere below him, and we have ropes strung out all over the cliff. It had been a lot harder climbing than we expected; the cliff was treacherously soft and crumbly, and the trees that seemed to offer inviting handholds turned out to be covered with thorns. Even the tree trunks had thorns.

I put a sling around a handy tree and clip myself into it, then try to figure out which rope goes to Tom, which ones to the boats. All these ropes make me nervous. I'm no climber. None of us are. I'm terrified that I'm going to unclip the wrong one and leave someone unbelayed.

"Send someone up!" I finally yell to Tom. Then I amend that: "Send Wick up!"

Some say that most expert whitewater paddlers are overgrown kids who have never managed to adjust to the adult world. Tom and I, both with children of our own, would still fit that description. But Wick Walker is clearly an exception. It's not just that he has a real career, as a major in the Army Corps of Engineers. It's a whole difference in attitude.

Trips like this, or the one to Bhutan in 1981, don't come off without someone willing and able to do the detail work, like obtaining and studying maps, making local contacts, taking pictures, and coordinating equipment. All of the dull

**Jamie McEwan navigates one of the Santa
Maria's drops. Photo by Wick Walker.**

things. It's handy to have an adult around, someone like Wick.

So it's a relief when Wick climbs up beside
me. Under his direction we change the belay and
start hauling the boats up. Soon the rope starts
to wear a groove in the soft limestone, increasing
the friction, and the boats hang up on small out-
croppings. For a while I just think of it as weight
training, a workout. That's while the outer layer
of skin on my hands lasts. When I get down to
the soft, pink underskin—with a few holes,

started by the thorns, all the way through to the
raw flesh—it gets harsh. Each boat comes up
more and more slowly. The last one gets stuck
near the top, and we go through three hard heaves
before we get it moving again.

Finally we belay Tom and Andy up. We're
nearly at the top of the waterfall.

We carry our boats over one more ledge into an
almost tropical forest. I'm the last, walking with
my head down, so I'm surprised to see their boats
suddenly on the ground before me. I look up. To

my right I see empty space, filled with the rising mist. Just on the brink of the waterfall is a circular, shaded pool, perfectly calm, blue, with a large tree growing up from its middle. Before me is the river, the Gallinas, sunlit, tumbling gaily over a series of small falls before taking its final plunge into the Santa Maria.

Grass and small flowers grow on tiny islands in the middle of the river. With the sunlight, the clear water, the shallow, splashing river, it's like paradise. Andy has stripped to his shorts and is swimming across the pool, completing the picture.

I sit down right where I am, pull the boat across my lap, and rummage through it till I find two candy bars: lunch. Heaven can wait.

We spend an hour and a half resting and exploring. Andy comes into his own at times like this: unaffected by the climb, he is everywhere; peering over the waterfall, swimming across the pools, exploring the feasibility of running the various rapids on the Gallinas.

I had arrived at the top feeling grumpy and sorry for myself, but between Andy's enthusiasm and the extra round of energy bars that Wick digs out of his boat (the first two didn't seem to reach my stomach—got diverted to another dimension, or something) I recover enough so that soon I too am wading and swimming. It is a magical spot.

But if we had stayed even another 20 minutes we might have been in real trouble. The descent is wooded all the way, not as steep as the climb, but steep enough that we have to use ropes. We work in pairs, Andy and I on one team, Wick and Tom on the other.

Andy and I reach the bottom first, at twilight.

It's a jumbled mass of boulders and carved rock; there is no good place to camp, so we walk downriver to scout the next rapid.

The added volume of water from the Gallinas has changed the nature of the river. The next rapid is not complex or tricky, but it's got plenty of raw power. The current banks off of one shore, slams into a large towering boulder, and rebounds into the canyon's vertical wall. It's getting darker by the minute and Wick and Tom are still descending the cliff.

I hike back up to the bottom of the cliff and shout up to Wick, explaining the situation.

"So, is it all right if we paddle on down and look for a campsite, before it gets completely dark?"

"No. Well—go ahead and paddle the rapid, but wait for us at the bottom."

There is something very spooky about paddling whitewater in the twilight. I follow Andy down the long, sloping approach to the rapid. The sensation of speed is much greater than in the light; dark shapes of rock move swiftly backward against the sky. The hissing of the water against the rock walls sounds very loud.

I pass through a chain of waves as I approach the drop. The water pushes me to the left as I drop over, the boulder is coming up, here is the wave coming off of it; it engulfs me, I lose control and flip. While upside down the bow of my boat hits the boulder, then I roll up—and here is the right shore, passing by.

I'm through. I feel more like a piece of driftwood than an experienced paddler in control, but who cares, I'm through.

Andy and I pull into an eddy below the rapid

Camping in the gorge of the Santa Maria. Photo by Wick Walker.

and talk quietly for a moment. The canyon is dark, its rock walls offering no place to camp, but there is still light and color in the sky.

"Tell you what," I say. "You paddle down and find a campsite, get a fire started; I'll hike back up and talk to Wick and Tom."

I climb and hike back upstream, using my flashlight to pick my way among the boulders. Wick and Tom have just arrived at the bottom of the cliff when I get there.

Wick doesn't seem too pleased about the idea of running the rapid in the dark. It's truly dark now; the stars are out.

"Well, you could portage, but it would be hard with the boats."

"Just shut off the light; let us get our night vision," Tom says.

I walk to the river's edge with them, show them where we put in. I tell them how to run the rapid.

I don't mention that it had knocked me over.

We stay up later than usual around the campfire that night, even though we know we'll have to cover 30 miles the next day. It should be an easy paddle, especially in comparison to what has come before. There is a feeling that the adventure is over.

We talk about the trip, trying to sort out the different days to fix them in our memories. It's hard to recall, hard to separate the miles of whitewater that flowed one into another. Instead, we identify the days by remembering the failures, the times we had to carry. Four portages on day one, including the long one where Wick had disappeared for a time under a jumble of boulders. Three on day two. None on day three, the day of what we called the "Maze Rapids." And only one, but what a one, today.

"You know," Wick says, "it was a good thing we had that climb thrown in there. Otherwise, it all would have been too routine."

"Yeah, and we wouldn't have seen the top of the falls," Andy adds.

I almost protest. My hands are throbbing, my back is sore, and we still have 30 miles to go. But then, maybe they're right. If being comfortable were our first priority, after all, none of us would be here.

Besides, I have learned a valuable lesson. Something I wouldn't have learned anywhere else. Nothing uplifting, or profound. Nothing earth-shattering. But simple enough to be passed along, to become part of paddling lore:

If you're going to scout a waterfall, bring along a diving mask.

URBAN CANOEING

By William G. Scheller   Illustrated by Barbara Carter

The snapping turtle lay motionless on the slick wet clay of the creek bank, a cranky, brooding chelonian with a cold and beady eye. I was standing in the creek, next to the canoe; Chris Maynard was clambering up the bank so he could size up our approach to the sixth fallen tree we had encountered in the last half-hour. The three of us—Chris, the snapping turtle and I—were isolated in a stew of berserk vegetation and warm brown water, a scant dozen miles from the White House.

To be specific, we were in Beltsville, on the grounds of the National Agricultural Research Center. But "grounds" is the wrong word, implying as it does some element of maintenance. The only force contributing to the maintenance of this pocket Amazon was the summertime climate of the North Temperate Zone, Middle Atlantic Division. It was wet, even in a nearly rainless summer, and the creek was full of sticker bushes and deadfalls, spiders that come to live in your canoe, water snakes and prehistoric turtles with toe-shortening jaws. It was a suburban no man's land,

the kind of junk wilderness that will never make it onto a protectionist's map but is wild nonetheless. It was the kind of terrain where you would expect to run into Flannery O'Connor's Misfit, the wacko in *A Good Man Is Hard to Find*. But we found not one single human anywhere during our first eight and a half hours on this creek. Some megalopolis! Paddling and dragging and thrashing along at half a mile per hour, we were invisible to the rest of the world and they to us, even as we passed beneath the Beltway.

But you're confused. Let me explain: The idea for this adventure was to canoe the Anacostia, Washington's unloved and rarely mentioned river, beginning to end. We do these things, Chris and I—go down dirty rivers in northern New Jersey or circle Manhattan in the filthy wakes of barges and excursion boats. So when we came to Washington, we didn't have in mind a paddle around the tidy Tidal Basin or a poke down the lovely C & O Canal. We like our rivers on the seedy side, running through cities and nondescript suburbs, and we go to great lengths to sabotage the

squeaky-clean, Hiawatha-in-the-forest image of the canoe.

Why? Why indeed. We make up different answers, of course, but basically there are two reasons: first, nobody else does it. Knock on wood, there hasn't been any big urban canoeing boom. This means you can paddle through Newark and see fewer people doing the same thing you are doing than you would if you were kayaking the Mackenzie Delta. Second, it gives you a matchless perspective on populated areas, one you don't get by car or on foot or by any other means of locomotion. Quietly canoeing through everybody else's workaday world creates a sense of being in one place and yet somewhere else at the same time. You glide along as if you were in a different dimension, as when we slipped under the Beltway. There we were, sharing the same approximate space as hundreds of automobiles and drivers, but they were on a highway and we were in a shady Maryland swamp. It's a sneaky business.

That's all very nice, of course, but someone will ask it: What were we doing under the Beltway?

The Anacostia doesn't get up that far. And, come to think of it, wouldn't it take a hell of a big tree to fall across it?

No, it doesn't, and yes, it would. But our purpose had been to start at the headwaters, to find the faintest trickle that could possibly answer to being the source of the Anacostia, launch the canoe in it, and head for the grand finale where the river merges with the Potomac in Southeast D.C. The big risk, as we saw it, would be the chance that in some sections the drought would have evaporated even the few inches of water needed to float a canoe.

With a sheaf of topographical maps and a day-long reconnaissance trip, we determined that the Anacostia, or at least its Northeast Branch, the Northwest being another story altogether, rises amid a tangle of nameless streams that crisscross the National Agricultural Research Center. The most accessible of these appeared to originate at a weedy pond on Soil Conservation Road; on the topo, it heads straight for the Baltimore-Washington Parkway and then merges with the other streams to form Beaverdam Creek. That gushing torrent ends at Indian Creek, just shy of the Beltway. Indian Creek then flows south through its namesake park, meets the Paint Branch at College Park, and finally earns the name "Northeast Branch, Anacostia" as it courses through Riverdale. At Hyattsville the Northeast and Northwest branches meet, and our river is officially the Anacostia. Then south it goes to the District, past the Kenilworth Aquatic Gardens (a national park of undeserved obscurity), RFK Stadium, the Sousa Bridge, and into the Potomac. To get there, canoeists, just follow the blue lines.

The whole trip figured to be between 15 and 20 miles. Given a nice early start and a decent water level, we expected to make landfall for a late lunch at the Capitol View Carryout on Pennsylvania Avenue, to nose past Fort McNair into the Washington Channel an hour or so later, and to arrive at our Maine Avenue hotel by *l'heure apéritif.*

As it turned out, the closest we came to liquid refreshment as the sun slipped toward the mizzen was a Coke machine on Greenbelt Road in Berwyn Heights. What undid our timing was not low water, although there was plenty of that on the gravelly open stretches south of College Park, but the hellish swamps and gloomy thickets of Beaverdam and Indian creeks. And the obstructions! But why do you suppose they call it Beaverdam Creek?

The first blue line we followed, the one that began on Soil Conservation Road at the head of the weedy little lake, disappeared after we rounded the first bend. Not behind trees, but into the ground, right after a beaver dam decorated with bottles and cans. The stream became mud, and the mud became skunk cabbage, and the skunk cabbage became a bramble patch. We found the point where it reappeared after half an hour of scouting and then dragged the canoe through the brambles like an ungainly sled. From there to the Beltway, strangely enough for this driest of summers, we usually had plenty of deep water, although it flowed through channels that were often six inches narrower than the width of our canoe, and were blocked every ten yards with the corpses of the trees that fall in the forest and nobody hears.

There are lots of ways to get around fallen trees. You can go over, which usually involves facing one another while straddling the tree, then hauling up the bow and passing the canoe forward; or you can go under, if the tree is high enough above the water. This maneuver is like doing the limbo in a canoe, while spiders crawl out of the tree bark and onto your face. Sometimes it's a tight fit. Whoever was in the bow would pop up and paddle forward gingerly, hoping not to hear a crunch and groan. Looking back does no good.

On two occasions the "under" maneuver served us well, when we had to duck cross-stream chain-link fences left mercifully high and dry by the drought. We were near Beaver Dam Road, and must have penetrated some off-limits part of the agricultural research facility. We never found out for sure. We were in between fences when a white station wagon stopped along the road, a hundred feet away. The guy got out and looked around. We crouched along the mud bank like two fugitive muskrats, peeking through reeds to see what was going on.

Finally, the USDA man, if that's what he was, got back into the wagon and left. We were free to discover the secrets of giant chickens and hardy new squash varieties.

It was very dark in the woods and swamps, and there were no sounds except the cries of birds once we were away from traffic. Deer tracks indented the stream banks, though we saw no mammals except each other and the man we had come to think of as the heavily armed agriculture cop. The only litter was whatever had floated down from the roadsides when the water had been high. There was a theme to this litter, and for a while it seemed that here, ten miles from the National Gallery and the Smithsonian Institution, our only link with civilization was a bobbing yellow plastic jug labeled with the single word "Prestone."

After seven hours of paddling and lugging and emptying our shoes of water that looked like tobacco juice, we stopped for lunch between lanes of the Beltway. Three and a half miles won so far. Chris pulled a leech off his leg. Up above, people who had left New Haven, Connecticut, while we were putting our canoe in the water zipped by.

After lunch, the hand of man finally intruded upon the Indian Creek environment in the form of a series of gravel pits. It was here that we anticipated the only high drama of the trip, because during our reconnaissance a few weeks earlier we had been told by a foreman at the gravel company that we wouldn't be allowed to navigate the chain of ponds that our maps said the stream would lead through. He was a fat man with piggy eyes and a dirty white shirt, red suspenders and a malevolent drawl. He looked as if central casting had sent him to play the final scene in *Easy Paddler*. But Billy Bob, as we had named him, never appeared. The maps were wrong, and Indian Creek never touched the gravel pit ponds.

Greenbelt Road, 4 P.M.: Here we hauled the canoe onto the bank beneath the bridge and hiked up into the Other World. At a gas station, we half-emptied a soda machine and phoned our car connection to revise our ETA in downtown Washington. Yes, Greenbelt Road, I told him. No, we'll make it. It's a nice clean paddle from here. We're out of the woods now.

And so we were. But from Berwyn Heights to Hyattsville was not so much a nice clean paddle as a long wet walk. The one thing we had dreaded, low water, was a fact in this channel-ized stretch of river. Seldom would we manage 50 feet of travel without having to get out and pull the boat along, like mules on the Erie Canal. This went on for nearly three hours, and, to make it worse, there was hardly anything to see along the way. This is not meant as an affront to the citizens of the lovely communities along the Northeast Branch, who no doubt enjoy their riverfront parks and find them quite picturesque. But they have the river to look at and, in times like these, the river bottom. If they were to try walking down the middle of the river, though, they would see nothing but its rip-rapped banks, a monotonous prospect after the first mile or so.

I could see it was starting to rattle poor Chris, who is a sucker for the built environment and takes pictures of it whenever he can. His photographic predilections, upended shopping carts and all, are the third reason we canoe through cities. I have a greater tree tolerance than Chris (as long as the trees are alive and upright), but even I was starting to burn out. In New Jersey, where I come from, they perk up the view along a river by building an industrial park every few miles.

The kiss-off to this part of the trip came from Toto the dog, a yappy little thing who belonged to a family that was dipping for tadpoles under the Decatur Street Bridge in Edmonston. I was towing the boat (lining, as the canoe people say); Chris was walking alongside. The mother looked at the two crumb-bum apparitions and then at her little daughters, but the old man was a jolly sort who called out "Not enough water, huh?" And then the dog took to our heels, barking and splashing as close as he dared. Dogged, we were,

on top of everything else. Finally the guy called him off: "C'mere, Toto."

". . . and your little dog, too," I muttered.

We reached the Anacostia itself—the real river, not some branch or tributary—at 7:20 P.M. In nearly 12 hours, we had come seven and a half miles. At least the walking was over. With each stroke, the paddles bit more deeply; soon we couldn't touch bottom at all.

Here, in Anacostia River Park, people were fishing. Farther north, where we had just come from, fish would have gotten sunburn. We saw carp jumping—"there's a million of them in here," a fisherman hollered from shore—but he and the others on the bank were angling for catfish. It wasn't rising fish that caught our eyes, though, as we glided past the Prince George's Marina and into the District at dusk. It was garbage: bottles, Styrofoam cups, fast-food boxes, all floating high in the water. The Anacostia here is an elongated dumpster, studded with bobbing junk. It's hard to tell where it all comes from, since both banks are almost entirely parkland. Do all Anacostia picnics end on such a note of abandon? Or does the stuff float up from downtown with the tide? One thing was sure—no First Lady ever has taken on the beautification of the Anacostia River.

Before we started this journey, we had figured on paddling into the Kenilworth Aquatic Gardens, accessible via a narrow inlet on the east bank. We'd read that there are giant lily pads in there, lily pads that can support a hundred pounds. I wanted to try two pads at once. Now, after 8 P.M., we had to let the inlet come and go. For diversion, we had to be content with an oil drum in the main channel. This was the biggest piece of flotsam we saw, although it might not have been the most unpleasant. Not ten feet away, four fingers of a heavy gray glove broke the surface. Whether the glove was empty, or even whether it was just a glove, was beyond our curiosity.

Now the shadows were falling fast. In the gloom along the east bank, the carcass of a '62 Oldsmobile nosed through the brush. The last of the evening's great blue herons settled onto a shoreside perch. Just ahead were the big stacks of a Pepco plant, with nicely kept grounds that descended to a perfect landing place. It was 8:45, and we were at the Benning Road Bridge. Even though we had covered the last three miles in a blind rush of one and a half hours, a pace we could easily have held in the broad, deep channel ahead, it was time to pack it in. Time to climb up and call for our ride. We were in Washington,

weren't we? Sure, we could have made the Whitney Young Memorial Bridge, and the Sousa Bridge, and the Eleventh Street Bridge, and even our original Maine Avenue destination—by midnight, we calculated. We could have made Newport News if we were crazy enough. After a while you wonder: What's the point?

The point, if we needed one to add to our usual excuses for urban canoeing, had already been made when we chose such an ambitious beginning. Launching the canoe in that ridiculous trickle up in Beltsville is what ruined our chances of a triumphant daylight arrival in the Washington Channel. But starting that far up and still paddling well into tidewater was what gave us whatever measure of accomplishment we had. Things might not turn out the way you plan; that's the risk you take. But you can start them any way you want.

SIERRA TRAVERSE

By Royal Robbins

From crystalline lakes fed by the snows of Mt. Ritter, the Middle Fork of the San Joaquin traces a serpentine course down the western slope of the Sierra Nevada. Sliding past Devil's Postpile, plunging over Rainbow Fall, it carves a deep and tortuous gorge around mighty Balloon Dome, finally spilling into Mammoth Pool Reservoir, a two-hour drive from Fresno, California.

Of all the virgin rivers in California, this one most attracted us because it would involve a *traverse* of the range. We would start on the east side, drive over Minaret Summit, and put in as high as possible, where the river is only a small stream. But an extra reward awaited us if we won through to Mammoth Pool. We would be not only the first humans to descend the river with boats, but the first to descend it, period. The smooth walls of the Granite Crucible around Balloon Dome had effectively denied passage even to rock climbers.

Reg Lake and I drove into Devil's Postpile Saturday, August 22, 1983 and spent the afternoon scouting the river. Next morning, we drove up canyon and then pulled our kayaks two miles to a creek emptying out of Shadow Lake. Because of downed trees, this is the highest possible put-in. We paddled six miles down this delightful stream, through pine and fir forests (unusual for California boating, which is done mostly in the foothills), and through mini-gorges of metamorphic rock. It was exciting to boat a river no one had experienced before.

A week later we returned, joined by our constant paddling friend, Douglas Tompkins. Doug had been away, and returned just in time for the fun. As teams go, we made a well-balanced one. Reg, bright, modest, and affable, was everyone's model boating companion. An expert kayaker, he mixed a love of adventure with a sound practical nature, and concern for the safety of his companions. Reg's skills made him the steering wheel.

Doug was the engine. His life has been filled with adventurous undertakings, from making important first ascents, running a guide service, snorkeling in the Red Sea, winning Class A ski

Royal Robbins becomes the first to descend the Double Chute, the last major obstacle
in the Crucible and the key to the success of the expedition. Photo by Reg Lake.

races, and flying a small plane several times between California and the tip of South America, to kayaking the wild waters of Chile and California. Doug's intense drive sometimes leads him to, but never over, the verge of recklessness. He is at home on the fine edge, and possesses a certain ineffable quality that enables him to get away with what, for someone else, would have been bad judgment.

In my 30 years of mountaineering, I had learned the value of marrying the romantic impulse for adventure to prudence. Lacking Reg's adroitness and Doug's strength and stamina, I was the natural choice to bring wisdom to the enterprise. Lacking even that, I contented myself with the job of brakeman, keeping the pace more leisurely so as to avoid the mistakes of haste. I also hoped that my special experience in the discipline of rock climbing would help the party in the granite canyon ahead.

As we prepared our gear early in the cool afternoon of August 29, visions of the test ahead danced in our heads. Doug and I reassured ourselves that we could rely on Reg to see us through. Reg, in turn, troubled by thoughts of being trapped in a canyon with unclimbable walls rising out of sight into the sky, was comforted by the realization that Doug and I knew what we were about when it came to climbing.

At the start, there was barely enough water to float our boats. This was the correct volume, because the gorges below would be impassable with a healthy flow at the put-in.

The section that Reg and I had boated a week earlier dropped an average of 75 feet a mile. This would normally be considered steep, but it was shallow compared to the rest of the run. The next 25 miles fell an average of 168 feet a mile.

We made three portages in the first three miles, including one around Rainbow Fall, which drops 100 feet into a pool of deep blue. We passed a memorable quarter hour here, sitting in our boats beneath this elegant plunge, reminiscent of Vernal Fall in Yosemite. Paddling up to it against a strong wind created by the cascade, we let the water thunder upon our heads, shoulders, and boats. It didn't occur to us, though we might have wondered, what would happen if a log came over.

A half mile later, we began the "Big Carry" to pass a gorge down which the water first drops 480 feet a mile and overall averages 400 feet for four miles. We had expected to carry the full distance, so we were astonished to find we could put in again after less than two miles. Darkness stopped us with one and a half miles of this first gorge left to go.

In the morning, we experienced a mile of fantastic boating—steep, but runnable, and very beautiful. But then we were faced with a gorge ending in a double waterfall: Waterslide Fall. We would have portaged if we could, but the east wall was unclimbable, and the west involved 3rd class rock climbing just to scout the rapid. Yet, to run the section above the fall, and get out before being swept over, was harrowing to contemplate. We spent two hours studying the problem, analyzing carefully our chances of running the rapid safely to reach the haven of a small eddy right next to the 80-foot fall. Finally, Doug went for it.

As Reg was climbing back to the put-in, Doug came through. I saw him come over the first drop with amazing speed. It hadn't looked that big, which made me wonder about the second drop, which Doug was already entering. He got lined up and plunged over, keeping his balance nicely in the four successive reversals in the drop. He

then turned on steam to cross the current and dart into the eddy. He would have been OK, but I grabbed his boat anyway. The lip of the falls was only 5 feet away.

My heart was pounding as I climbed back around, and down to my waiting kayak. As I climbed across the wall, 150 feet above the turbulence, I saw Reg getting into his kayak. I missed his run because he was then hidden from view, but as I reached my kayak, I saw that he and his boat were safely out of the water by the falls. Two down, one to go. I was daunted by the combination of the steep, narrow canyon, the tough rapids, the brief pool and even briefer eddy, and the lethal plunge of the fall waiting as a result of the slightest error. I knew I could do it. It was just a question of control. First of all, self-control, and then control over the kayak. As I slowly fastened the spray cover over the cockpit, I told myself, "You're *going* to do it." I realized, as I pushed into the current, that I was scared. The first riffles were stronger than expected. The water was moving more rapidly, curling over and around rocks, forming small reversals. Then it converged to the right before dropping sharply left into the pool below. As I sped toward it, I realized that the drop was bigger than I had thought. I careened left, and a new menace showed itself: half of the water shot directly into a rock spike which could be a wrecker. I was correctly positioned, and avoided the rock by passing on the right.

The water was now blocked by large rocks, except on the far right where it cascaded down in a modified "L." The bend was not as sharp as I had earlier thought, but on the other hand, this was no place to get stuck broadside in the narrow, steep, convoluted chute. It was, as we had guessed, a hard grade IV. As the waves came first from one direction and then from the other, it was necessary to correctly anticipate the pitch of the boat and to brace at the right moment on one side and then the other. Failing to do this would make the curl leap over the side of the boat, causing a capsize. A capsize halfway down meant hitting rocks upside down and a possible swim, perhaps with injuries, which would in turn lead to a plunge over Waterslide Fall.

The curls came first from the right, then the left, then the right again. I stayed loose, braced, and plunged into the pool. With my eyes fixed on the little harbor where my friends were waiting, I gave a few quick strokes and drove my boat across the current into safety.

We had a quarter-mile carry here to rejoin the river a bit above Fish Creek, a tributary almost as large as the Middle Fork itself. On that second day, we boated only four miles. The gradient averaged 225 feet per mile. The river was now running between 200 and 300 cubic feet a second (cfs).

The third day was the easiest. The gradient was down to 125 feet a mile. This meant more boating and less carrying, and we were able to enjoy the excellent rapids and wilderness scenery. The water of the North Fork had now been added, increasing our flow to 400 to 500 cfs. We went six miles that day and camped at the Cassidy Bridge, about two miles below Miller's crossing.

The next section, four miles long, was like kayaking through a Xanadu wonderland, involv-

Rainbow Falls, a 100-foot drop where the kayakers sat beneath the plunging water. Photo by Royal Robbins.

**Doug Tompkins coming over the 12-foot drop of Arrowhead Falls into the pool above
Double Chute in the middle of the Crucible, the crux of the trip. Photo by Reg Lake.**

ing the Cyclopean Bathtubs, Measureless Caverns, and the Great Corridor, before reaching the South Fork.

The Bathtubs are a series of quiet pools interrupted by sharp drops. The walls rise in bathtub curves, unbroken by a single crack, and sometimes only two kayak widths apart. In the Measureless Caverns, the river disappears completely beneath a gigantic jumble of boulders.

The Great Corridor is formed by the San Joaquin tracing a path around massive Balloon Dome, its granite walls rising 2,900 feet directly from the sparkling green water. The Corridor itself is divided into Granite Gorge, the Crucible, Giant's Elbow, and Boulder Dams. The crux is the Crucible. It has four sections: First Falls (around which we had to climb and rappel into the pool below), Arrowhead Drop, Double Chute, and Last Drop. We were nearly stopped by the Double Chute, because it was impossible to scout. But Reg saved the day with a daring climb from his kayak onto a slippery boulder right next to the drop. From his vantage point atop the rock, Reg's voice, even though he shouted hoarsely, had a poetic ring to our ears as he confirmed, "It'll go!"

We made our fourth and last camp at the South Fork, having descended that day 650 feet in four miles, an average drop of 150 feet a mile. After the South Fork, the river carried 600 to 700 cfs. On the fifth day, we struggled through the last gorge via drop-pool rapids formed by huge rockfalls, and after five miles reached the wind-swept waters of Mammoth Pool.

There are a lot of rivers harder than the Middle Fork of the San Joaquin, and a lot of kayakers more skilled than we three. But by a combination of luck, teamwork, and skill, we had achieved a unique success. In terms of a climbing counter-part, it reminded me of the Salathé Wall on the flank of El Capitan in Yosemite. When we made the first ascent in 1963, we felt the same fear and joy of adventure, the same battling with the impersonal elements of nature, the same need for technical skill, and the same awestruck wonder at the glory of the handiwork of God. Like the Salathé, the San Joaquin trip was a perfectly rounded adventure. It had a beginning, a middle, and an end, and took place in an incomparable setting. It certainly was the kayak trip of our lives.

FIRST BEND ON THE BARO

By Richard Bangs

Above, the jungle was a brawl of flora and vines and roots. Colobus monkeys sailed between treetops, issuing washboard cries.

Below, three specially designed inflatable whitewater rafts bobbed in a back eddy, looking, from the ridge, like restless water bugs. There were 11 of us, all whitewater veterans, save Angus. He was in the raft with me, John Yost, and Karen Greenwald. As the leader and the most experienced river runner, I was at the oars.

Our raft would go first. At the correct moment we cast off—Angus coiled the painter and gripped for the ride. I adjusted the oars and pulled a deep stroke. For a prolonged instant the boat hung in a current between the eddy and the fast water. Then it snapped into motion with a list that knocked me off my seat.

"This water's faster than I thought," I yelled. Regaining the seat, I straightened the raft, its bow downstream. The banks were a blur of green; water shot into the boat from all sides.

Just minutes after the start of the ride, we approached the rapid. Though we'd been unable to scout it earlier, I had a hunch that it would be best to enter the rapid on its right side. But the river had different notions. Despite frantic pulls on the oars, we were falling over the lip on the far left.

"Oh my God!" someone screamed. The boat was almost vertical, falling free. This wasn't a rapid—this was a waterfall. I dropped the oars and braced against the frame. The raft crashed into a spout, folded in half, and spun. Then, as though reprieved, we straightened and flumped onward. I had almost gasped with relief when a lateral wave pealed into an explosion on my left, picking up the raft, slamming it against the nearby cliff wall like a toy, then dumping it and us upside down into the millrace.

I tumbled, like falling down an underwater staircase. Seconds later, I surfaced in the quick water below the rapid, a few feet from the overturned raft. My glasses were gone, but through the billows I could make out another rapid 200 yards downstream, closing in fast. I clutched at a rope and tried to tow the raft toward the shore.

Behind, I heard Karen: "Angus. Go help Angus. He's caught in a rope!"

He was trailing ten feet behind the raft, a piece of the bowline tight across his shoulder, tangled and being pulled through the turbulence. Like the rest of us, he was wearing a sheathed knife on his belt for this very moment—to cut loose from entangling ropes. His arms looked free, yet he didn't reach for his knife. He was paralyzed with fear.

With my left hand I seized the rope at his sternum, and with my right I groped for my own Buck knife. In the roily water it was a task to slip the blade between Angus's chest and the taut rope. Then, with a jerk, he was free.

"Swim to shore," I yelled.

"Swim to shore, Angus," Karen cried from the edge of the river.

He seemed to respond. He turned and took a stroke toward Karen. I swam back to the runaway raft with the hope of once again trying to pull it in. It was futile: The instant I hooked my hand to the raft it fell into the pit of the next rapid, with me in tow.

I was buffeted and beaten by the underwater currents, then spat to the surface. For the first time, I was really scared. I saw another rapid speeding toward me. Abandoning the raft, I stretched my arms to swim to shore, but my strength was sapped. This time I was shot into an abyss. I was in a whirlpool, and looking up I could see the surface light fade as I was sucked deeper. At first I struggled, but it had no effect, except to further drain my small reserves. My throat began to burn. I went limp and resigned myself to fate. In the last hazy seconds I felt a blow from beneath, and my body was propelled upward. I was swept into a spouting current, and

at the last possible instant I broke the surface and gasped. I tried to lift my arms; they felt like barbells. My vision was fuzzy, but I could make out another rapid approaching, and I knew I could never survive it. But neither could I swim a stroke.

Then, somehow, a current pitched me by the right bank. Suddenly branches and leaves were swatting my face as I was borne around a bend. I reached up, caught a thin branch, and held tight. I crawled to a rock slab and sprawled out. My gut seized, and I retched. A wave of darkness washed through my head, and I passed out.

When my eyes finally focused, I saw figures foraging through the gluey vegetation on the opposite bank. John Yost was one—he was a close friend since high school. Lew Greenwald, another. He had been in the third boat, and seeing him reminded me that there were two boats and seven people behind me. How had they fared?

John paced the bank until he found the calmest stretch of river, then dived in; the water was so swift that he reached my shore 50 yards below his mark. He brought the news: The second raft, piloted by Robbie Paul, had somehow made it through the falls upright. In fact, Robbie was thrown from his seat into the bilge during the first seconds of the plunge, and the raft had continued through captainless. The third boat, handled by Bart Henderson, had flipped. Bart was almost swept under a fallen log, but was snatched from the water by the crew of Robbie's boat.

All were accounted for—except Angus MacLeod.

The date was Friday, October 5, 1973. I was 23 years old. The place was Ilubabor Province, Ethiopia, and our goal had been to make the first raft descent of the Baro River, a major tributary of the White Nile. We had come here, all of us, at my design: I had graduated from the Colorado River and spent four summers guiding rafts and tourists through the rapids there, all the while dreaming of far-off waters. Inspired by accounts of the British army making a raft descent of Ethiopia's Blue Nile in 1968, I'd set my sights on Africa. But where the British had failed—one of their party, Ian MacLeod, drowned while attempting to cross a swollen tributary—I felt certain I could succeed. It had struck me before that Angus had the same surname as the British fatality, and I even mentioned it to Angus, but neither of us was superstitious.

In February of that year—1973—with a small team of conspirators, I had made the first descent of Ethiopia's Awash River. A month later we repeated our success on the classic Omo, a river famous to the world because of Louis Leakey's fossil discoveries on its lower reaches. Both expeditions pitted us against a litany of obstacles, from hippos and poisonous snakes to crocodiles and deadly microorganisms in the water. It was the crocodiles we feared most, so we named our venture SOBEK Expeditions, after the ancient Egyptian crocodile god of the Nile. I had returned to the Colorado with tales of exotic river running, and now, along with three Africa veterans, seven newcomers had followed me back to tackle another river—the Baro.

As a fervid river runner, I felt I understood the reasons for everyone's involvement in the expedition, except Angus's. He was the odd man out. I'd met him in New Jersey a few weeks before our departure. We were introduced by a neighbor of his, whom I'll call Tom. Tom liked to tell people that he was a "professional adventurer." He'd had a brochure printed up, describing himself as "Writer, Scientist, Adventurer, Ecologist." Something about him seemed less than genuine, but he had hinted that he might invest in our Baro expedition, and we desperately needed money. I agreed to hear him out. He flew me from Arizona, where I'd been guiding, to New Jersey. I was impressed—no one had ever offered to pay air fare to hear my plans, and Tom's family certainly had money. In exchange for what seemed like a sizable contribution to our cause, Tom had two requests: that he be allowed to join the expedition, and that I consider letting his friend, Angus MacLeod, come along as well.

I was leery of bringing along anyone outside my tightknit, experienced coterie on an exploratory, but the lure of capital was too strong. Tom, however, would never make it out onto the Baro. He traveled with us to the put-in, took one look at the angry, heaving river, and caught the next bus back to Addis Ababa. He may have been the smartest of the lot.

Angus was altogether different. While Tom smacked of pretension and flamboyance, Angus was taciturn and modest. He confessed immediately to having never run a rapid, yet he exuded an almost irresistible eagerness and carried himself with the fluid bounce of a natural athlete. He was ruggedly handsome and had played professional soccer. After spending a short time with him I could see his quiet intensity, and I believed that—despite his lack of experience—he could handle the trip.

Once in Ethiopia, Angus worked in the preparations for the expedition with a lightheartedness that masked his determination. On the eve of our trip to Ilubabor Province—a 17-hour bus ride on slippery, corrugated mountain roads—

I told Angus to make sure he was at the bus station at 7 A.M. for the 11 A.M. departure. That way we would all be sure of getting seats in the front of the bus, where the ride wasn't as bumpy or unbearably stuffy. But, come the next morning, Angus didn't show until 10:45. He got the last seat on the bus and endured.

Later, after the accident, standing on the bank of the river with John Yost, I wondered if I'd made the right decision about Angus. We searched the side of the river where I'd washed ashore; across the rumble of the rapids we could hear the others searching. "Angus! Are you all right? Where are you?" There was no answer. Just downriver from where I'd last seen him, John found an eight-foot length of rope—the piece I'd cut away from Angus's shoulders.

After an hour John and I gave up and swam back across the river. We gathered the group at the one remaining raft, just below the falls.

"He could be downstream, lying with a broken leg," someone said.

"He could be hanging onto a log in the river."

"He could be wandering in a daze through the jungle."

Nobody suggested that he could be dead, though we all knew it was a possibility. All of us had a very basic, and very difficult, decision to make, the kind of decision you never want to have to make on an expedition: Should we stay and look for Angus, or should we get out while there was still light? Robbie, Bart, and George and Diane Fuller didn't hesitate—they wanted out. Karen Greenwald wanted to continue searching, but she was hysterical and the weakest member of the group. Against her protests, we sent her out with the others.

That left five of us—Lew Greenwald, Gary Mercado, Jim Slade, John Yost, and me. We decided to continue rafting downstream in search of Angus on the one remaining raft. I had mixed feelings about it—suddenly I was scared to death of the river; it had almost killed me. Yet I felt obligated to look for a man missing from a boat I had capsized, on an expedition I had organized. And there was more: I felt I had to show something to the others—that I wasn't scared of the river.

But the river wasn't through with us. When we were ready to go, I climbed into the seat of the raft and yelled for Jim to push off. Immediately we were cascading down the course I'd swum earlier. In the rapid that had nearly drowned me, the raft jolted and reeled, kicking Gary and me into the brawling water.

"Shit—not again," was my only thought as I spilled out of the raft into another whirlpool. But this time I had the bowline in hand, and I managed to pull myself quickly to the surface. I emerged beside the raft, and someone grabbed the back of my lifejacket and pulled me in. My right forearm was lacerated and bleeding. Jim jumped to the oars and rowed us to shore.

My injury wasn't bad—a shallow cut. But Gary had dislocated his shoulder; he'd flipped backward over the gunwale while still holding onto the raft. He was in a lot of pain, and it was clear he couldn't go on. Lew—thankful for the opportunity—volunteered to hike him out.

John, Jim, and I relaunched and cautiously rowed down a calmer stretch of the river, periodically calling out for Angus. We were just three degrees north of the equator, where the sun sets promptly at 6 P.M. year-round. It was twilight when we approached another large rapid, so we decided to stop and make camp. It was a bad, uncomfortable night. Between us, we had a two-man A-frame tent, one sleeping bag, and a lunch bag of food. Everything else had been washed into the Baro.

The rude bark of a baboon shook us awake the next morning. The inside of the tent was dripping with condensation, and we were soaked. I crawled outside and looked to the eastern sky, which was beginning to blush. My body ached from the previous day's ordeal. I wanted to be back in Bethesda, at my folks' home, warm, dry, and eating a fine breakfast. Instead, we huddled around a wisp of fire, sipping weak tea, and chewing wet bread.

The next morning we eased downriver, stopping every few minutes to scout, hugging the banks, avoiding rapids we wouldn't have hesitated to run were they back in the States. At intervals we called into the rain forest for Angus, but now we didn't expect an answer.

Late in the afternoon we came to another intimidating rapid, one that galloped around a bend and sank from sight. We took out the one duffel bag containing the tent and sleeping bag and began lining, using ropes to lower the boat along the edge of the rapid. Fifty yards into the rapid, the raft broached perpendicular to the current, and water swarmed in. Slade and I, on the stern line, pulled hard, the rope searing our palms, but the boat ignored us. With the snap of its D-ring (the bowline attachment), it dismissed us to crumple on the bank and sailed around the corner and out of sight.

There was no way to continue the search. The terrain was too rough, and we were out of food, the last scraps having been lost with the raft. We struck up into the jungle, thrashing through wet, waist-high foliage at a slug's pace. My wound was becoming infected. Finally, at sunset, we cleared a near-level spot, set up the tent, squeezed in, and collapsed. Twice I awoke to the sounds of trucks grumbling past, but dismissed it as jungle fever, or Jim's snoring.

In the morning, however, we soon stumbled onto a road. There we sat waiting, as mist coiled up the tree trunks. In the distance we could hear the thunder roll of a rapid, but inexplicably the sound became louder and louder. Then we saw what it was: 200 machete-wielding natives marched into sight over the hill. General Goitom, the police commissioner of nearby Motu, hearing of the accident, had organized a search for Angus. Their effort consisted of tramping up and down the highway—the locals, it turned out, were more fearful of the jungle canyon than we were.

I remember very little of the next week. We discovered that Angus had held a United Kingdom passport, and I spent a fair amount of time at the British embassy in Addis Ababa filling out reports, accounting for personal effects, and communicating with his relatives. John and Jim stayed in Motu with General Goitom and led a series of searches back into the jungle along the river. We posted a $100 reward—more than double what the villagers earned in a year—for information on Angus's whereabouts. With financial assistance from Angus's parents, I secured a Canadian helicopter a few days after the accident and took several passes over the river. Even with the pilot skimming the treetops, it was difficult to see into the river corridor. The canopy seemed like a moldy, moth-eaten army tarpaulin. On one flight, however, I glimpsed a smudge of orange just beneath the surface of the river. We made several passes, but it was impossible to make out what it was. Perhaps, I thought, it was Angus, snagged underwater. We picked as many landmarks as possible, flew in a direct line to the road, landed, cut a marker on a dohm palm tree, and headed to Motu.

A day later John, Jim and I cut a path back into the tangle and found the smudge—a collection of leaves trapped by a submerged branch. We abandoned the search.

Three months later I was wandering through the recesses of the spice market in Addis Ababa when a vendor I knew approached me. "Mr. Richard. Did you hear about Mr. Angus? They say he is alive. He was found by villagers on the river, and he is living with them now. It is the talk everywhere. I do not know from where the story comes."

I went to the British and U.S. embassies. People there, too, had heard the rumor. One consul said he'd heard a fanciful embellishment to the story—that Angus was living fine and well as king of a tribe of Amazon-like women. As the story went, Angus had been visited by outside villagers and invited to leave with them, but he'd declined. He was in Paradise.

Hearing the rumors was hard. I wanted to squelch the sensational gossip, to finish business left undone, to determine beyond all doubt what had really happened to Angus. And to cleanse my conscience. So in January of 1974, I made another trip to the upper reaches of the Baro. This time the river was ten vertical feet lower than on our last trip: It was dry season in a drought year. What was before a swollen rampage was now a slow, thin trickle. There were four of us in a single raft: Lew Greenwald, Gary Mercado, Professor Conrad Hirsh of Haile Selassie University, and me.

Again, we reached the first rapid within minutes. This time, though, it was a jumble of bus-sized basalt boulders, the bedrock that fashioned the falls during times of flooding. It was unnavigable, so we stood in chest-deep water and wrenched the inflatable boat over and down the rocks, turning it on its side to push it through the tighter passages. A similar configuration constituted the next rapid, and the next, and the next. The routine was quickly established. It was a constant battle against rocks, water, heat, fatigue, and insects. We had naively hoped to run the raft some 150 miles to Gambella, near the Sudanese border, where the river flows wide and flat. We had rations for a week. With all the portaging, we were making less than five miles a day.

Scattered along our course, sometimes in branches high above us where the water once swirled, we found vestiges of the first expedition: five oars, Jim Slade's sleeping bag, a torn poncho, a pack of insect-collecting equipment donated by the Smithsonian, crushed pots and pans, and a ripped sweater that had belonged to Angus, one he had packed in his duffel. But no sign of Angus.

After six days we had made only 30 miles; our bodies were pocked with insect bites, and we had exhausted our food and strength. A trail up the steep slope put an end to our ordeal. We repaired to Addis Ababa with no new answers.

I returned to the States and graduate school, running few rivers myself but continuing to manage the business of SOBEK (which was growing despite the accident) from my apartment. The following January, Lew Greenwald, my original partner in the business, was drowned on an exploratory run of the Blue Nile in northern Ethiopia. The news shattered me: I burrowed deeper into academia, denounced river running as selfish and insane, and put SOBEK aside.

Time softened my edges. By summer I had re-enlisted and was once again organizing trips to Ethiopia—though I had no intention of ever going back myself. But the mystery of Angus gnawed. Sometimes in the middle of a mundane chore —taking out the trash, doing the laundry—I'd stop and see Angus's frozen features as I cut him loose. In weak moments I would wonder if there just might be a chance that he was still alive. And I'd be pressed with a feeling of guilt, that I hadn't done enough, that I had dishonorably waded in waist deep, then turned back. I wondered how Angus had felt in those last few minutes—about himself, about me.

In November of that year, 1975, I got a call from a friend, a tour operator. A trip he'd organized to the Sahara had been canceled by the Algerian government, and his clients wanted an alternative. Would I be interested in taking them to Ethiopia? Two weeks later I arrived in Addis Ababa, where I met up with John Yost, Jim Slade, and a trainee-guide, Gary Bolton, fresh from a SOBEK raft tour of the Omo River. They were surprised to see me, here where nobody expected I would return.

By late December, after the commercial tour, John, Jim, and I had decided to try the Baro once again. The river pummeled us, as it had before, randomly tossing portages and major rapids in our path. But during the next few days, the trip gradually, almost imperceptibly, became easier. On Christmas morning I decorated a bush with my socks and passed out presents of party favors and sweets. Under an ebony sapling I placed a package of confections for Angus. It was a curiously satisfying holiday, being surrounded by primeval beauty and accompanied by three other men with a common quest. No one expected to find Angus alive, but I thought that the journey —at least for me—might expunge all doubt, exorcise guilt. I wanted to think that I had done all that was humanly possible to explore a death I was partly responsible for. And somehow I wanted him to know this.

As we tumbled off the Abyssinian plateau into the Great Rift Valley of Africa, taking on tributaries every few miles, the river and its rapids grew. At times we even allowed ourselves to enjoy the experience, to shriek with delight, to throw our heads back in laughter as we bounced through Colorado-style whitewater and soaked in the scenery. Again, we found remnants of that first trip —a broken oar here, a smashed pan there. Never, though, a hint of Angus.

On New Year's Eve we camped at the confluence of the Baro and the Bir Bir rivers, pulling in at dusk. A lorry track crossed the Baro opposite our camp. It was there that Conrad Hirsh, the professor from the second Baro attempt, had said he would try to meet us with supplies. We couldn't see him, but Jim thought there might be a message waiting for us across the river. "I think I'll go check it out," he said.

"Don't be a fool," John warned. "We're in croc country now. You don't want to swim across this river."

An hour later, just after dark, Jim had not returned. We shouted his name, first individually, then as a chorus. No answer. Jim had become a close friend in the two years since we had shared a tent on the upper Baro; he had been a partner in ordeal and elation, in failure and success.

Now John and I swept our weak flashlight beams along the dark river. We gave up. We were tired, and we sat around the low licks of our campfire, ready to accept another loss, mapping out the ramifications in our minds. Suddenly Jim walked in from the shadows and thrust a note at us.

"Conrad arrived three days ago, waited two, and left this morning," he said, his body still dripping from the swim.

"You fool! I knew you couldn't disappear now —you owe me $3.30 in backgammon debts." I said it with all the disciplinary tone I could muster.

The following day we spun from the vortex of the last rapid into the wide, Mississippi-like reaches of the Baro. Where rocks and whirlpools were once the enemy, now there were crocodiles and hippos. We hurled rocks, made threatening gestures, and yelled banshee shrieks to keep them away. Late in the day on January 3, 1976, we glided into the outpost town of Gambella. The villagers there had neither seen nor heard of Angus MacLeod.

I never told Angus's relatives of our last search; we didn't find what might have given them solace. What I found I kept to myself, hidden like buried treasure in my soul. It lies there still, dusty, but ready to be raised if needed. It is the knowledge of the precious and innate value of endeavor. Both Angus and I tried, and in different ways we both failed.

I hardly knew Angus MacLeod, not as friends and family know one another. But in the years of searching, wondering, I've gotten to know him in other ways. There are things we tell ourselves. I want to believe that when Angus boarded my tiny boat and committed himself, he was sparked with life and light, that his blood raced with the passion of existence—perhaps more than ever before.

On that first Friday in October, 1973, ten of us thought we knew what we were doing: another expedition, another raft trip, another river. Only Angus was exploring beyond his being. Maybe his was a senseless death, moments after launching, in the very first rapid. I will never forget that look of horror in his eyes as he struggled there in the water. But there are other ways to think about it. He took the dare and contacted the outermost boundaries. He lost, but so do we all, eventually. The difference—and it is an enormous one—is that he reached for it, wholly.

Finally, though it took years, I believe I did the same.

The source of the Braldu, a stream trickling down the surface of the 31-mile-long Baltoro Glacier. Masherbrum, 25,660 feet high, is in the distance.

KAYAKING IN THE KARAKORAM

Photos by Galen Rowell   Text by Bo and Kathy Shelby

The Braldu River flows from the glaciers of the the Karakoram Range of the Himalayas, the world's greatest concentration of high mountain peaks, including K2. This is a wild, harsh land whose uncompromising nature is matched only by its incredible beauty.

In May of 1984 we paddled the Braldu with Andy Embick, Rob Lesser, and Bob McDougall. Photographer Galen Rowell, on assignment for the National Geographic Society, went along to document the trip from shore.

We reached the put-in with the help of Balti porters, carrying our boats upstream along the river's 60-mile length to an elevation just over 11,000 feet. The steep-walled valley contains beautiful carved rock as well as the rubble of old glacial moraines clinging high above the river. Falling rock, an objective danger to which kayakers are unaccustomed, injured one of the porters.

Spring had arrived in the tiny villages along the lower part of the river. Some villagers here nurture crops in small, steeply terraced fields; others work as porters, hoping to save enough to open small shops. The people were friendly and unabashedly curious, crowding around to see what marvels of technology would emerge from our packs and to find out what we intended to do with the brightly colored plastic things that most of them did not recognize as boats. A few remembered the unsuccessful 1978 British expedition that killed leader Mike Jones, or Dave Mamby's 1983 attempt that ended with his near-drowning after a vertical pin.

At the put-in, the Baltoro Glacier ends in a wall of ice several hundred feet high. The river roars full-grown from a carved blue cavern, carrying giant icebergs broken off from the face of the glacier. The rapids are long, continuous stretches of wild whitewater, plunging into steep, narrow chutes, crashing into vertical walls. Occasionally the river disappeared into strainers formed by house-sized boulders, forcing us to portage on the slippery rock walls. We were able to run the river on a spring flow of 1,000 to 2,000 cubic feet per second. By late June, snowmelt swells the river to a raging torrent ten times this size, ren-

A Balti villager from Dassu carries a
kayak for 40 rupees ($3) per day.

Kathy and Bo Shelby in a placid part of the Chokpo-Chongo
Gorge just before the river plunges through the Narrows.

dering all but the easiest sections unrunnable.

The kayaking was difficult and technical; so was the photography. To keep pace with us, Rowell often had to race up the steep walls to detour around a rocky obstacle, then race back down to the water to catch us. In the Chokpo-Chongo Narrows—where the river enters a dark, sinuous canyon, spanned high above the water by a footbridge only eight feet long—he literally hung by a rope to get the shots he wanted.

Bob MacDougall running a Class 5-plus section of the Chokpo-Chongo Gorge
that Embick and the Shelbys chose to portage. No place to eddy out.

Kayakers leave the Braldu Narrows, where the
river is forced between walls of overhanging rock
10 to 20 feet apart for a quarter of a mile.

THE HOOKMAN

By Timothy Hillmer

Cruz remembered the first time Old Crawdad took him down to the river with the hooks. *Like throwing a shotput underhanded on a string*, he had told him. *Ain't no picnic being a hookman. Dead bodies is heavy at the bottom. They'll fight ya.* Crawdad's voice was raspy, like a creaking hinge being shut on a cage, and he dangled the hooks at his side as casually as a string of trout. Ten pounds of metal-pronged claw attached to thick gold-line rope. He showed Cruz how to coil the line, then belay it out after he'd thrown as the barbed talons dragged along the bottom in the tugging current.

"Never tie it on," Crawdad said, "or you'll be as dead as the ones you're looking for. Drag you right under."

Cruz listened to him, balancing the hook in one hand. He kept three loose coils of the heavy rope in the other, then began to rock back and forth, swinging the grappler like a pendulum gaining momentum. When he released, the hook flew like a steel bouquet, soared in a wide arc, and plummeted into the river.

"Keep the line taut so's you can feel for something catching. You'll pull up a lotta shit, kid. Branches. Pieces of scrap iron. I hooked a kitchen sink once. Thought I had Moby Dick under there."

He showed him the gloves. Black leather with extra padding sewn into the palms and extending halfway up the forearm to prevent rope burns.

"You'll know when ya got one," said the old man. "There'll be this thump on the line, and then it's like they're crawling up the hemp all of a sudden, coming up after ya, the hook caught in their chest or leg."

He drove him along the river and showed him the best places to look, where the strong eddies carved out pockets in the shore and the current reversed upstream. Near Trout Bridge. Across from Hobo Campground. In the tangle of trees parallel to the abandoned mine.

"I learned all the good fishing holes. I pulled up six in one summer." Crawdad laughed and Cruz saw a flash of black gums. "It's not pretty, kid. Spooky line of work."

He needed the money. He had to pay rent and buy groceries and take care of his father, Tucker, who was on the wagon. They lived in a trailer in the alley behind the Shady Lane Saloon. Two bedrooms and a bath. A mattress on the floor for each of them. Cruz kept the blinds drawn so the dust would stay out. Tucker liked it that way. Dark.

It was the only work he could find since getting laid off in Bakersfield. Kern River Search and Rescue was the official name. They wore yellow hard-hats and khaki shirts with the brown and green Forest Service logo emblazoned like a tattoo on their sleeves. Fires up in Sequoia. Cars going off the road from L.A. and into the canyon. Cleaning up the shore after the motorcycle gangs had partied. It was mostly river work on the Kern. A tourist tangled up in a snag at midstream. Fishermen with their legs trapped in rock cracks. Hunting for bodies after a drowning. They lost six to eight each summer, usually during the high water. Someone would get too close, slip, and they'd be gone in the froth of white. Two days later the body might wash through the gorge. Sometimes it took months.

Cruz was the new boy on the team. He was younger and stronger than the others, barely 17, so he handled the hooks. The veterans didn't touch rookie work. They drove the trucks and gave orders to the newcomers. They'd done their time and liked to talk about it. Especially Walker. Cruz listened to the stories he told.

"Pulled a biker out from under the bumper of a Mercedes in my first week," Walker said. "Skull crushed and head split open like a coconut. I zipped him up in the plastic and let the EMTs haul him away. I went behind my jeep and threw up in the ditch. Get out if ya don't like it."

It was the sound of the telephone Cruz dreaded.

Sometimes the calls came long after midnight, and it was as if he'd been sweating and waiting hours to hear Lou, the boss, say "brush fire" or "rockslide." He'd rehearsed in his mind what it would be like the first time he dragged the river. Two A.M. Phone rings. Lou will say in a croaking wheeze to meet at Miracle Springs. "Another one, kid," he'd say casually, as though he were ordering a second round of drinks. "Fell in below the dam. Found some tennis shoes. A carton of bait. Probably some rich geek from L.A." Geeks. Cruz hated the word. That's what they called the dead ones. Cruz had never seen a geek. The others joked with him about it. "Just wait," they said, "your turn'll come."

The work kept Cruz busy. Landslides over the roads in the high country. Nothing serious. They started sandbagging in May for the high water they knew was coming. There had been a big snowpack at Mt. Whitney and the river would swell soon, icy water rushing down from the Sierras in a torrent. Walker made bets with the others on the first geek.

"Before the middle of June," he'd say, "put your money down. All proceeds to the Geek Funeral Parlor."

Cruz never bet. It disgusted him. They called him "rookie" and "greenhorn." He kept his distance. They kidded him about other things. His old man. Mostly women and his inexperience with them.

It was the last week in May. Dark night. No stars and clouds swirling in. Cruz was in bed listening to his father groan in his sleep, staring at the clock, when the phone rang. He knew it was Lou.

"Looks like Walker won his bet, kid," he said. "Tourist thinks he saw a guy fall in. Found a jacket and camping gear. Porsche parked near the Springs. Water's hauling ass. We'll have to hustle to get him out before he gets into the gorge. Bring your hooks.''

When Cruz arrived, the others were already fanning out, methodical, as though they were walking to church. He went with Crawdad below Trout Bridge. The hooks were heavy, clanking together in the silence. When they reached the bank he saw the river, all foam and whirlpool, slamming into a jam-up of willows and scrub brush.

"Good spot," he heard Crawdad say. "Good place to get hung up."

Cruz was sweating when he threw the first one. The hook rose straight up and then bounced in the shallows.

"Shit, kid," the old man hissed, "get it out in the meat of the water where it counts. Ain't much time. No mercy in that river."

He threw again, a good one this time, and he felt the rope slide through his fingers. The current was strong, sucking the claw down into the violent flow and away from him in seconds.

"Work your way down like I showed ya," he heard Crawdad say. So he did, dragging the steel across the bottom toward the jam-up, the black gloves hot from the friction of hemp on leather.

They worked nonstop for two hours, Crawdad shining the light, Cruz throwing the hook. A rhythm began. He'd measure the distance, toss the grappler, haul it in. A few snags, mostly wood or rock caught in the webbed talons. Water glistened on the black steel. He felt Crawdad's breath on his neck when he threw, the light flashing over his shoulder and tracing the arc of the hook through the air. Crawdad was eager. He watched for a sudden tension in the line. A trembling. A

pulling down. Cruz smelled whiskey on his breath.

It was near dawn, the sky like slate, when the hook caught. Cruz felt the change in the rope, heard Crawdad's breath quicken.

"He's down there, kid," he said. "I know these things." The hook came free and they tried again, this time throwing upstream and letting the claw drift down. Three attempts and nothing grabbed.

Cruz was scared. He wanted to get away from the river, to run and let Crawdad finish this. He wanted the hook to break off or the rope to snap. But the old man was there, pressing.

"He's stuck on something," he mumbled. "Work fast. He might get away." They continued, trying to relocate where the obstruction had been in the riverbed, each time the hook sinking down into the oily dark and then pulled in, empty.

The line went taut on the ninth try. Cruz felt it slithering away from him and down. The weight was moving under there, shifting, the swift current trying to tear it loose. Crawdad helped him, their arms straining to bring it in. Breath puffed out in short gasps. Legs shook. Cruz wanted to cut it, let it go, but Crawdad pulled on, his eyes fixed on the line and the point of descent. They felt the rope jerk suddenly, the weight breaking free and inching downstream. Their feet slid in the mud toward the water.

"Dammit, tie it off!" yelled Crawdad. "Wrap it around something!" Cruz let go briefly and secured the rope around a tree trunk. For ten minutes they heaved at the line, hauling it in against the force of the river. Forearms throbbed. Fingers cramped.

Then he saw it. A bare shoulder breaking the surface. A head, the scalp pink and shining in the light. A hand, limp and bent against the current. They pulled the body into the shallows. Crawdad held the line. Cruz went in after it.

Cold skin. Like fingertips on a freezer wall. The smell enveloped him. Not death. River scent. When he grabbed the shoulder to ease it out of the shallows, he saw a torn red t-shirt. Jeans, now heavy with water. He picked the body up in his arms and set it on the bank in the high cutgrass.

Crawdad shined the light down. Cruz saw a woman. Young. Maybe 23.

"Look at her skin," Crawdad said. "Hardly been touched. Only dead a few hours. Like she's sleeping."

Cruz saw closed eyes. Lips parted as in mid-dream. The face was pure and milky, as if scrubbed by sand and water. Cruz thought of the chalky smooth face of a statue in church. He put his hand on her cheek, in her hair, over her eyelids. Pure. Like moist cotton. As if one touch could bring her back. One kiss. He felt his eyes blur, his stomach twist. Then Crawdad's hand on his shoulder.

"The first is the hardest, kid. Go easy. Let's wrap her up." But Cruz couldn't and stumbled away. So the old man covered her in the tarp. They drove back to the others, Cruz not saying a word.

June brought the heat. It descended on the Kern like a veil of flame. Cruz put in 12-hour days in the 100-degree weather. The snowpack near Whitney broke all records and each day the river inched further above the high-water mark as the sun melted the mountain glaciers and fueled the torrent. They sandbagged along the bridges and near the riverside cabins and homes. Eighty-pound bags stacked six to eight feet high. "Ball-breakers," Crawdad called them. When that was done they started on the firebreaks up in Sequoia, tearing out sage and cactus with picks and shovels, always listening for the sharp buzz of a rattler's tail. The forest was parched and crisp, ready to burn. Crawdad was on their asses no matter what.

"Flood or fire, water or smoke," he'd sing out, "it's hot as Hades and you're working like ladies."

Crawdad was always there, like a devil on his shoulder. Teaching him. Cussing him. His silver hair hanging from under his stained hat like tassels. Cruz knew nothing of his history. No wife. No family anyone knew of. Only the river and forest for as long as anybody could remember. Cruz trusted Crawdad's knowledge of the land and liked the way ke kept Walker and the others at a distance. Liked his vulture nose. The whiskey smell of his breath. The acrid, sweet scent of the little Dutch Masters cigars he smoked.

"Two packs a day for 20 years," he'd howl, "and lungs like snow."

The daily grind took everything out of Cruz. He came home to the cramped trailer, his skin like scorched copper. Tucker was usually asleep in his room, the faraway sound of the Dodgers game on the radio. Cruz would shower, then rub lotion on his raw skin. The heat took away his appetite. He drank glasses of iced ginger ale to kill the bitter taste of sand and dust in his mouth.

At night he hauled an old air mattress on top of the trailer and slept under a gulf of stars. He imagined a cool breeze drifting inland from the Pacific to soothe him from the heat. In the distance he could see the twitching pink and green neon of the Kern Valley Motel. He listened to the sound of traffic out on the interstate. He dreamt of the drowned girl.

In the dream she was alive and staring up at him with eyes like black eels, her mouth so close he could feel her breath on his lips. Looking down he saw the hook thrust into her side and the blood seeping into the cutgrass like syrup. He awoke suddenly, cursing the dream, feeling lost and adrift in an ocean of death and night and darkness. All he knew was her name. He had read it in the newspaper obituaries. Denise Kaufmann. Age 19. Born in Bakersfield in 1960. Both parents deceased. No surviving family.

There were no drownings in early June, so Cruz didn't work the hooks. They rattled in the back of Crawdad's truck like a skeleton. But within two weeks the Kern rose 2,000 cubic feet per second and Cruz saw the river transformed into a raging torrent of foam and power. The search and rescue team went on 24-hour alert, and they eyed the bridges and highway embankments carefully as the silt-laden waters clawed the shoreline. They posted DANGER signs in the parks and campgrounds and warned tourists to stay away from the Kern.

One evening he drove his old man's jeep down to Hobo Campground. The riverside trailers had been abandoned and left to the mercy of the flooding. *A ghost town*, thought Cruz. A stray dog sniffed at an overturned garbage can. Water lapped at the wheels of an abandoned truck. From the shore he could see giant willows that had collapsed into the river and floated downstream, their roots and foundations eaten away by the powerful current. A few trees had jammed up in a boulder garden and created an enormous strainer to sift the river like a gold dredge.

He sat near the river's edge and watched the sleek water rush by, glassy and green as jade. He liked the sound it made—"sweet music" Crawdad called it—and the way it enveloped him and blocked out all other sound. He could feel the coolness rising off the surface, cutting the heat like a razor. He thought of the drowned girl and wondered whether her death had been a suicide. He thought of Crawdad and the hooks and wondered if the old man inquired about the past lives of those he dragged from the river. He sat there until the Kern faded in the dusk and the water became a stream of gleaming oil rolling in front of him and his mind felt cleansed of sweat and work and dust. This was all he needed. This sweet music, endless and eternal, flowing into the canyon below.

On the morning the Kern peaked at 7,000 cfs, Lou called a meeting at headquarters. It was midweek and Cruz was dreading another three days of chopping out cactus and mesquite in the high country. They gathered in the corrugated steel warehouse behind the main office, and Cruz spotted Crawdad standing off to the side, squinting out from under his baseball cap.

"I need a couple of men for the river rescue team," Lou began. "Saunders and Martinez, the core crew, quit on me yesterday and moved up north. I need volunteers to use a raft and oars to rescue stranded swimmers or search the shoreline for bodies. I received word this morning that the river ain't going down for awhile, that there's enough snow up near Whitney to keep it high until damn near August."

He paused, shifting his weight from one boot to the other.

"With the big water here to stay," he continued, "we might as well gear up for some accidents. Any volunteers?"

Cruz could hear Walker and the others talking in the corner. Then there was a long silence, interrupted only by the roar of a gravel truck passing by outside. Lou cleared his throat and spoke again.

"How 'bout it? I need some help here."

Walker spoke first. "None of us vets gonna touch that job. No way in hell, Lou. We done our time. Besides, that goddamn river's suicide right now."

Lou stared at the crowd, his pudgy face ragged and sweating in the heat. He started to say something, but stopped, only to turn and stare away for a moment. Then Cruz saw a hand go up from the side of the crowd.

"I'll help out," Crawdad said, "but I'm too old for this shit. I need somebody to row."

Cruz felt his skin tingle when he heard Crawdad, a layer of quiet settling over the group. He could feel the old man's eyes on him and he looked down at his feet. He knew what the others were thinking. He was the new kid, the greenhorn. He and Crawdad were alike in that they had no wives or children, no real family but for his father. Cruz knew he had paid no dues, at least not like the others. He looked up and saw Crawdad still glaring at him, waiting for him to step forward and back him up. He thought of their time by the river and the way the old man had taught him to use the hooks, the way he had covered up the drowned girl when Cruz couldn't stomach it. He felt his face redden, heat up. He raised his hand.

"OK Cruz," said Lou. "You and Crawdad get the river gear. Training starts this morning and . . ." Walker's voice cut him off in midsentence.

"I ain't saying this cause I wanna take the kid's place, but the Kern's no place for rookies. Especially now. The kid don't know shit about what he's getting into. The rapids down there will eat him alive. Hell, nobody should be going near that river. It's a death trap. Why should we die cause some geek falls in? I say let 'em drown."

Then Cruz saw Crawdad step into the pack of men. He spoke directly to Walker. "Why don't you ask Cruz what he thinks?"

Until then Cruz had felt like an outsider, a spectator. But suddenly he felt the focus of the crowd shift to where he stood.

"What do you say, boy?" said Crawdad. "You heard Walker say what he thinks. Now it's your turn."

The old man's gaze was unblinking, intense, and Cruz could see his red eyes waiting for an answer. He knew what Crawdad needed from him this time, just as he'd known when they'd gone to the river with the hooks. But he let the dark weight of the question hang in the air for a moment, let the silence fill the space between him and the others like a wall.

"You can back out," Crawdad urged him. "I'll find someone who ain't afraid. You decide." He could feel the old man pressing again, could hear his words haunting him. *Ain't much time . . . no mercy in that river.*

"I ain't afraid of the Kern," Cruz said. "Besides, somebody has to go out on the river. It might as well be us."

Then Crawdad turned to Lou. "He'll know his shit when I'm done working with him, boss. He'll know his shit or we'll both drown like fucking rats in the willows, and I don't plan on dying soon. Didn't he take on the hooks when nobody else wanted them? Didn't he?"

"You can sign his ass goodbye," said Walker, striding out of the warehouse and away from them.

Cruz heard a buzzing of voices around him, then saw Crawdad approaching. "Don't listen to Walker," the old man told him.

"He's a first-class bullshit artist. C'mon. Stay close and I'll make a boatman out of ya."

"Geek Patrol" was what Crawdad called it in the beginning. Cruz felt scared that first morning, Walker's words still fresh in his mind, as they drove down to some slow sections of the Kern where the river opened up out of the willows. Crawdad dragged from the truck the old boat, a 16-foot black military raft, and stretched it out in the sand.

"It's old," Cruz said.

"Shit," Crawdad said, "it's old alright, but it's hauled too many bodies out of the river to go under now. It's a fucking river hearse. Look at this."

He showed Cruz the grey, rectangular patches checkering the seams and tubes. Cruz ran his hands along the rough surface, feeling the irregularities as if they were zippered scars against his fingertips.

"You sew up a raft just like a man," Crawdad said. "There's needle and thread under all these rubber Band-aids."

Then the old man took a bucket of river water and washed the boat down until the black exterior shone like sealskin. They took turns inflating the six chambers with a cylinder pump, going at it until Cruz could feel his forearms and back throb.

They unloaded the ten-foot oars, each one sleek and heavy as a wooden beam in Cruz's arms, and set them next to the raft. There were other things in the back of the truck. Rusty ammo boxes, smelling sour and dank when the lids were popped off. A metal rowing frame with a slanted wooden seat attached. Frayed coils of rope wound tight as a hangman's noose. Two thick plastic body bags for drowning victims. "Corpse condoms," the old man called them. All of the gear carried the scent of mildew and decay, like items unearthed from a long storage underground. The musty odor filled Cruz's nostrils with an awareness of the tools and their trade. To carry the dead from water to an earthen grave.

Crawdad taught him the knots, the sheet bend and bowline and trucker's hitch. At first the rope was awkward in Cruz's fingers, like stiff wire in the hands of a child, but the old man stood beside him and guided his hands through the invisible patterns. They used red webbing to lash the steel frame into the center of the raft, cinching it down taut to the metal D-rings. They slid the boat into the river and tied it off to a tree, then watched it bob and sway in the green current. Crawdad slid two of the oars into the U-shaped metal oarlocks jutting skyward from either side of the frame, then showed Cruz how to lash the third to the side.

"Once you've learned to row, she'll be like a black bullet in the whitewater," Crawdad said.

He made Cruz begin that morning at the oars, sitting in the wooden slantboard rowing seat. "Be careful how ya slide, or you'll get splinters up yer ass," he told him. He called it a crash course in river sense, in learning to row by rowing. "Sometimes you got to be a fucking fortune-teller.

That's what it takes. Seeing the unseen," he said.

The oars were bulky and awkward in Cruz's hands and he struggled, catching the wooden tips on rocks or thick roots buried in the shallows. The river was deceptive, even in the calm sections. The swirling undercurrent twisted the oar blades flat beneath the surface and they plunged down, ripping Cruz forward as he clutched the handles and was nearly jolted from the boat. He flailed impatiently at the river, hoping the oars would bite into the water for a powerful stroke. He felt overwhelmed and frustrated that first morning, as if the Kern were conspiring to trick him at every turn.

Crawdad showed Cruz how to feather the blades as they dipped back into the water so they would slice through the emerald current like fins. He taught him the basics: the pivot, the double-oar turn, the portogee. "Use yer legs more!" he'd shout. "Drive up with yer legs. That's where yer power is." The old man was like a barking demon, always positioned directly behind Cruz in the stern of the raft. "Pull with the left oar . . . too hard, dammit! Correct with the right. Keep the angle. Now point yer bow at the shore and pull away. Don't lose it. PULL!"

For a week they worked the slow stretches, ferrying back and forth across the current, practicing angle pivots and catching the calm pockets of water behind boulders. Cruz would go home at night with quarter-sized blisters on his palms. He bought leather gloves and cut the fingers off to protect his hands when he rowed. The old lifejacket he wore chafed his skin raw under the armpits, and his lower back was inflamed with pain after the first day. But he learned to relax at the oars and listen to Crawdad. "You're picking

it up fast, kid. A natural. Let the river do the work for you. Go with the flow."

Soon he grew accustomed to the icy tingle of water lapping at his ankles in the morning, the itch of poison oak breaking out on his skin. Slowly, the river world became more to him than just a place of the dead. The days of working the hooks and sandbagging and digging firebreaks up in Sequoia seemed long ago, replaced with a sense of timelessness, of watching a wave curl endlessly back and repeat the sharp cycle of water and its motion. Each morning revealed blue sky and a gold wafer of sun slanting down from the canyon rim as they rigged the raft. When he felt the river streaming beneath the boat, taking over, he sensed a childlike electricity within himself, like gliding across stormy waters on a magic carpet.

During the second week they moved downstream to where the river narrowed. "Ya gotta dance like a water bug down here," said Crawdad. "Dance or drown." He called this section "the jungle." Willows arched out over the river, their roots stabbing up through the surface, the water boiling as it slithered in and out of the tangled foliage along the shore. The rapids had been christened by Crawdad with names like Strangler, the Cauldron, and Executioner. They all contained short bursts of frothing waves within tight channels. "The trees are the killers," he heard Crawdad say one morning at put-in. "Get pinned underwater by a willow and the water'll hold you there till Christmas."

The undercurrents and twisted passages of the jungle were like a frightening maze of traps for Cruz. He grew afraid each time he felt a sudden burst of speed as they accelerated blindly around a bend; each time the dark water tugged the raft toward a partially submerged mass of vines and branches; each time Crawdad's voice jumped him from behind and began to screech commands. When they stopped at noon for a brief lunch, Cruz ate little. His mouth tasted sour and his stomach churned at the thought of what lay downstream. He yearned for the hot afternoons of digging firebreaks in rattlesnake country.

Crawdad showed little mercy, continually pushing and correcting his every stroke. When they reached Nightmare Corner later in the day, he even refused to describe the rapid beforehand as he had with the others. "You're on your own," he said. "I ain't always gonna be around to look out for ya. Read it and run it."

Looking downstream, Cruz saw a series of cresting waves surging into a tangled stand of low-hanging willows on the right. He pointed the stern of the raft left and began to pull away from the trees, but the first powerful wave crashed into the boat, spinning it backwards and out of control. Cruz strained at the oars, trying to pivot the boat back around as they descended into the rapid, when suddenly, he heard Crawdad scream "DOWN!" Too late, he felt something solid and heavy explode into the back of his head like a hammer and he was swept into the river.

Dazed, he saw water swirling around him, endless and deep. *I am drowning*, he thought in a panic. *This river is my grave.* Then he felt iron hands on the collar of his lifejacket as he was ripped from the depths and thrown onto the floor of the raft. Choking, he spit out water and panted for air. He looked up and saw Crawdad at the oars, grinning as he rowed the boat away from the willows.

"You OK?" Crawdad asked. "That was one helluva branch that decked ya."

"I think so," Cruz answered. His head pounded, and he felt a walnut-sized swelling on the back of his neck.

"You're lucky, kid. Brother Blue Heron was smiling on ya today. Those willows aren't usually so merciful."

"Brother Blue Heron?" Cruz repeated, puzzled.

"Hell," Crawdad cackled, "he's king of the river gods and protector of all boatmen. But you can't know Brother Blue until the river kicks yer butt at least once. And you've just been baptized!"

They both began to laugh, softly at first, then louder. Cruz could feel the adrenalin seeping away, tension easing into the air.

"You're crazy," he said to the old man. "Crazy as hell."

"Maybe so," said Crawdad, "but I've had a lot of close calls on the river and Brother Blue always brought me back up for air. Now get yer butt up here and row."

Cruz clambered over the thwart and switched positions with Crawdad. As he began to maneuver the boat downstream, he said, "Thanks for grabbing me."

"You're welcome," said Crawdad. "Maybe you'll do the same for me someday if the river gods are with us."

"And Brother Blue Heron," said Cruz.

"And Brother Blue," echoed Crawdad.

In the weeks that followed there were other accidents. A drunken motorcyclist plunged his Harley 100 feet off Lover's Leap into the Kern. A six-month-old infant was swept out of the hands of a preacher while being baptized near Trout Bridge. Each time Cruz was called out with the hooks, he waited for the task to get easier, for the victims to become faceless in his dreams. By the third body he knew he could never cleanse his memory of the dead. *All victims whose time has come,* Crawdad liked to say. *All resting with Brother Blue.*

On the last Saturday in June Cruz's old jeep broke down. He had to hitchhike to Kernville to the auto parts store for a new fan belt. By the time he headed back to Lake Isabella on the Reservoir Road, it was late afternoon and the sky had darkened to a plum color in the west. He stood by the roadside, keeping an eye on approaching vehicles as well as the distant storm.

An old man gave him a ride in the back of his truck to Bodfish, then vanished up into the hills in a cloud of dust. *Probably a miner,* thought Cruz, one of those desert rats who emerge from their hideouts once a month to check the P.O. Box and get a drink. For ten minutes he stood by a Dairy King drive-in, his thumb out, watching as the motor homes and other tourists passed him by.

He recognized the red Bronco truck from a distance and immediately dropped his thumb, then turned his back as the vehicle came closer. Cruz heard the squeaking of brakes as it slowed beside him. He looked over and saw Walker's red face, a veil of sandy hair thinly pasted to his scalp.

"I thought it was you," Walker said. "Where you headed?"

"Back to Isabella," answered Cruz. He held up the fan belt. "My jeep's on the blink and I had to get this in Kernville."

"Hop in. I'm headed that direction."

Cruz walked reluctantly to the door and climbed in. The Bronco was luxurious in comparison to his jeep. Cool air hissed from the side vents. The seats were clean and shiny. Emmylou Harris crooned from the tape deck.

"Nice," Cruz said.

"Thanks. It gets me around."

"So where you been?" Cruz asked.

"I had to visit my ex-wife in Kernville and see my little boy. Saturday-only visits are a bitch, but I love to play with the kid. He's a slugger. Seven years old and already he hits like Garvey."

They were silent for a while, just listening to the tape. Cruz was glad for the music. He felt uneasy around Walker, especially after the confrontation in the warehouse with Crawdad.

"So you're working a lot with the old man?" said Walker.

"Yeah."

"I heard you pulled that biker out last week. Sounded like a pain in the ass."

"Three hundred pounds and then some," said Cruz. "Took us four hours to get him in. He was snagged in a brush pile."

"I know how it is," said Walker. "I was on the hooks when I started with the Forest Service."

"How long ago?"

"About eight years. I put in my time with Crawdad. I'd watch that old fucker, if I were you. Don't trust him. He's crazy."

"How's that?" asked Cruz.

"Him and his Brother Blue Heron bullshit. He's obsessed with that river. Did you know he pulled his own daughter out with the hooks back in the fifties? Some said it was a suicide. His wife left him afterwards. Nobody talks about it anymore. You'd think he'd be scared to death of the Kern.

The old guy ain't together anymore. Cracked up. Lou said they've caught him stealing from the dead. Rings. Watches and bracelets. Garcia caught him red-handed with a victim's wallet."

Cruz was silent after that. They were drawing close to Lake Isabella. A raindrop splattered on the windshield and trickled down. He wasn't sure if he could believe Walker. As they came down a hill he could see that the streets in town were already wet and slick with a glaze of warm rain.

Within five minutes they were pulling up next to the trailer behind the Shady Lane.

"Thanks," said Cruz.

"No problem," replied Walker. "Hope the belt fits."

Cruz hesitated before getting out. "He's not all crazy. He knows the Kern like no one else. He's taught me things."

"I know," said Walker, "but watch yourself. Don't let him get you into something you're not ready for. His life don't mean shit to him. He's hanging on with a bottle of whiskey."

"Thanks for the warning."

He got out of the Bronco, then watched as Walker pulled away and vanished down the alley. He stood there for a moment in the rain, thinking about what Walker had said. He tried to picture Crawdad with a wife and daughter a long time ago. He saw a different man, a father pulling his dead child from the river. *The first is the hardest*, he had said to him, *go easy*. He took it all in. The dust turning to mud at his feet. The laughter slipping from the back door of Shady's. His heart pounding as if encased within a tin statue. Then he walked inside thinking of the jeep and the fan belt and the dinner he would make for his father. Then sleep. His time to dream. His sweet music.

A storm front moved in on Friday morning during the first week in July. The early morning was overcast, the sky darkening with deep shades of purple and charcoal. Lou called Cruz at 4 A.M., startling him from sleep.

"I just heard," he said. "Crawdad called. Says he was coming up the canyon from Bakersfield last night, when a Mexican family flagged him down near Hobo. Said their son was missing. Meet Crawdad at Manning's Bridge. Take the raft and hooks and search the willows. Kid might be pinned and still alive, so hurry. No time to waste. Storm's coming."

They were on the river by dawn, rescue gear and ropes lashed tight into the boat. They brought the hooks, storing them in a thick canvas bag and tying it to the rowing frame. Cruz felt a chill when he touched them, the prongs rust-tipped, like blood dried and baked from the sun. They wore faded yellow raingear under their lifejackets, smelling damp and sour. Cruz rowed the jungle section again, working hard at the oars until he felt sweat inching down his ribs. He saw the river now as a narrow ribbon of landmarks he had memorized and learned. The buffalo-shaped rock perched like a high sentinel on a cliff, marking the entrance to Executioner Rapid. The hermit's abandoned cabin near Trout Bridge. The powerhouse at Borel. Thunder rumbled south near Bakersfield and he glimpsed jagged veins of lightning flashing like the edges of broken glass.

Crawdad sat behind him, saying little. Both Cruz and the old man knew the water might rise with the storm, maybe up to 7,500 cfs or more. Crawdad studied the shore and the strainers for the missing boy as Cruz focused on the river. They worked their way down methodically, hopping from one side to the other like a zig-zagging water strider, Crawdad's disjointed finger pointing the way. There were moments when Cruz imagined he was alone and rowing in solitude. Then he would hear a rasp behind him, a voice of warning.

"Be ready, boy. There's a family waiting to know if their kin is drowned or alive. Sweating it out. This ain't no time for relaxing."

When the rain came it felt like pearls of ice on his cheeks. "Manna from the river gods" is what Crawdad might have called it. *Answered prayer from Brother Blue*, thought Cruz.

It was drizzling when they reached the towering granite wall near the take-out. It was streaked with mineral deposits, each strand a tributary of color. Cruz began to ease the boat over to shore when Crawdad stopped him.

"Not here. We're going further down today, where the river's tighter. More places to get hung up. Just you row. I'll take care of the fishing."

Cruz hesitated, letting the oars drift free in the water.

"I've never seen this section before," he said.

"Don't matter," said Crawdad. "I know it well. I can talk you down it."

"Shouldn't we get back-up from shore?"

"No time for that. Brother Blue's telling me the kid's down further. I know it."

Cruz could feel a drumming inside his chest. *Watch yourself*, Walker had said. He silently longed for Crawdad to spot the body before they went further into the canyon. He had not even seen this lower section from the road high above. Shielded by an overhanging shelf of granite, it had always been a place of shadows for Cruz, a dark slit in the landscape where the river narrowed. A no man's land.

In the first half mile the tangled foliage of willows and scrub brush gave way to vertical sheets of granite and basalt slanting down to the lip of the river. No sign of a body. Then the rapids began. "Asskickers," Crawdad called them. Cruz had never seen water so huge. White-tipped waves poured over the bow, filling the boat as Crawdad scooped out the muddy water with a plastic bucket. Cruz could feel the pulse of the current quicken beneath the raft, as if the streambed were tumbling down a staircase of time-hewn steps. They were descending now, going deeper. No roads or take-out beaches visible. The rain fell in shimmering torrents, turning the walls into fortresslike slabs of ebony. Water spilled from the cliffs above, cascading in great streamers and pumping the river with speed. Cruz felt the raft dive into the trough of a wave, then rise up and break through as if at sea in a storm.

He looked for places to pull over and climb out. There were none. He silently cursed the old man for bringing him down here. He struggled to follow his directions, the whitewater a blur of motion. The main rapids came at them in dark succession and the old man summoned them by name: White Maiden's Walkaway, Sundown Falls, Deadman's Curve, Silver Staircase; all twisting, blind drops where the river suddenly plummeted down into violence. Oddly, Cruz thought of history lessons he'd read as a child, how the early explorers were told the earth was flat and to sail off the edge was to perish in hell. *To where dragons wait* was the warning echoing in his mind as he approached each horizon line, trusting only Crawdad's words as to what lay below.

The day seemed timeless, water billowing like white fire around them. The boat was sluggish to maneuver, brimming full with the icy river. The rest places near shore were few, and the Kern whipped by in a racehorse blend of enormous suck holes and razor-sharp rocks. At Coffin Corner, the black raft slammed against an undercut boulder, wedging tight, and water began to pour over the upstream tube, threatening to wrap the boat like cellophane around the obstacle. Cruz and Crawdad threw their bodies against the downstream edge of the raft. They strained against the onslaught of water. Suddenly the boat popped free and they scrambled back to their positions, Cruz at the oars and Crawdad bailing. He felt his forearms tighten and grow numb from gripping the oar handles. He was at siege with the fury surrounding him.

They reached Gravedigger Falls late in the afternoon. Still no sign of a body. Crawdad made him pull the boat over to scout this one. Walker's warning loomed clear in Cruz's mind. He was uncertain of everything now, even Crawdad's story about the Mexican family and the body. *Don't trust him*, Walker had said. *He's crazy*. But maybe Walker had been lying in order to disgrace the old man and keep them off the river. Cruz saw no clear choices. They had made it this far. He would go the rest of the way.

They tied off in the trees and hiked down along a slippery ledge. Cruz saw a gleaming, V-shaped tongue of glassy water sliding into the rapid like an arrow, the entire entrance overshadowed by a towering wave at the bottom. One hundred yards downstream the river vanished between two black monoliths of granite.

"This here's just the little brother," yelled Crawdad above the roar, pointing at the wave. "Down below is Gravedigger Falls, the big daddy deathtrap. No way are we going into that. I seen a kayaker try and run it once. His boat came out in pieces. Never found the body."

He was silent for a moment, almost reverent as he stared at the horizon line downstream. "We'll pull over just above it on the right and portage. There's a footpath we can carry the boat around on. Only one way to run Gravedigger Falls. On shore."

His directions for the rapid in front of them were straightforward. "This little one's called Tombstone. No way to portage it. You gotta break through the lateral waves coming off the right, then keep pulling to slip by the big curler at the bottom. Maybe I'm getting too old for this shit, kid, but don't go near the left. Stay clear of that bottom wave. Hit it dead on and we'll flip. If the river sucks you down into the falls, you're a drowner for sure."

As they hiked back to the boat, Cruz felt his mouth suddenly go dry as sand. He had no spit. He paused, letting Crawdad get ahead of him so he could stop and pee, all the while listening to the deafening clamor of the rapid. Doubt clouded his mind. Simple thoughts of self-preservation, of not wanting to die. *His life don't mean shit to him*, Walker had said. He stopped at the water's edge and closed his eyes, smelling the dank scent of rotting wood, feeling his breath escape in shallow, uneven gasps. He longed for sunlight and warmth. He imagined being at the top of the canyon and peering down into shadows, down into the abyss where he now stood.

He walked back to the raft where Crawdad waited.

"Walker told me you were crazy," Cruz said.

"Fuck Walker," Crawdad replied.

"Isn't this crazy?" Cruz said, pointing at the river. "I mean, look at this rapid."

"It's crazy if you don't think you can do it." He fixed Cruz with a questioning stare. "What's the matter, boy? Are you doubting Old Brother Blue now when you most need him? Are you pissing on the legend?"

"No."

"What else did Walker tell you?"

"Nothing else," Cruz said angrily, "but why haven't we found the body?"

"Because there is a body and there ain't," said Crawdad. "There is if you believe Old Brother Blue and all he's taught you and why we're here. There ain't a body if you believe that lying bastard, Walker. Which is it?"

"Untie the boat when I'm ready," was all Cruz said.

They launched from the trees after Crawdad had bailed the boat dry. The current was sleek, accelerating, and Cruz hung close to the shore, the raft's stern pointing right. Twenty feet above the drop he began to sweep hard on the oars, gathering momentum to break through the first lateral waves of the tongue. Suddenly he felt the raft glance off something, perhaps a finger of rock jutting up from the shallows or a root. In a flash, Cruz saw the boat rebound out into the center, then careen sideways into the maw of the rapid. He felt dizzy, a sickening emptiness in his stomach as his oars flailed madly at water.

"Straighten it!" he heard Crawdad shout, and he did, a last-second pivot swinging the bow around before they rocketed into the bottom wave. Cruz saw the black raft peel upward like a dagger pointing at the sky, straight and true, only to be buried by a colliding wall of darkness.

Flipped, he thought, stunned, as he tumbled helplessly, head over heels, out the back of the boat. Like being in a washing machine filled with black ink, the muddy water forced its way in and pummeled him. He grabbed for a line, the raft, Crawdad's hand. Only churning water. In his nose. Throat. He felt himself spun upside down. He saw the fading surface light, the air bubbles exploding around him. He was dragged under as the current sucked at his lifejacket, pounded him in the depths, then hurled him up again. He clawed for air. *No mercy*, thought Cruz, as he was flung down into a white chamber of foam. *Geek*.

Then he felt a surge, a downward thrust, like being shot from a cannon, and his body was flushed away, released. He broke the surface directionless, choking, the air like ice in his throat. The waves broke over him and he began to swim toward what he thought was the right shore, his hands knifing through the water as the bulky raingear and lifejacket dragged in the current. He kicked through another wave, then lunged ahead, groping for a rock, a tree limb. He felt a stone outcropping and muscled his way up, crawling onto his stomach until he was out of the river, safe on shore, hacking water from his flooded lungs.

Crawdad? He whirled and saw the black raft upside down and hurtling away from him downstream. He could see the old man clinging to the perimeter line on the side, tugging at it as he tried to pull the boat to shore. *Crawdad held on*, he thought as he watched the raft hovering near the entrance to Gravedigger Falls. "Swim!" he screamed. Then, too late, he saw Crawdad, his faded lifejacket still visible as he hung frozen on the horizon line for an instant, vanishing into the foam spitting up from below. Gone. Off the edge of the world. *To where dragons wait.*

He perched on the rock, staring at the empty void where Crawdad and the raft had been only seconds earlier. He expected to hear a scream, a shout of fear or pain. Nothing. Only the roar. In shock, he got to his feet and began to stumble along the shoreline, his heart pumping within the frail inner cave of his chest. A feeling of helplessness overwhelmed him. He was aware that Crawdad could be trapped downstream and he could not reach him. Cruz saw the haunting image of the boat disappearing over the ledge, Crawdad's head snapping back. Cruz gasped for breath, panic humming in the air like a swarm of insects buzzing relentlessly around his head.

He scrambled over car-sized boulders, his tennis shoes heavy with water. He slipped on the wet stone, fell down, then rose to climb again. He wasn't sure how long it took to reach the rapid. Time seemed not to exist in this moment. Only distance. He struggled up a granite slab to its crow's nest pinnacle. What he saw was breathtaking.

A white maelstrom. At the top the river narrowed into a tight channel, then spilled 30 feet down into a gigantic cauldron of thrashing waves and reversals. In the center of it all loomed a towering fang of rock, a basalt tooth with geysers of spray billowing off the sides. It was as if some demonic force beneath the streambed had suddenly erupted into a tempest.

He couldn't survive this, Cruz thought. *Nobody could.* He scanned the rapid for signs of the boat or Crawdad. At first there was nothing, only raging water. Then he saw a single oar, seemingly unbroken, jutting up from the river like a mirac-ulous golden staff, shaking violently. Upon looking closer, Cruz saw it had been driven down into a rock crack and imbedded like a chisel into marble. He searched for a flash of orange or yellow, any sign to reveal that Crawdad might be trapped somewhere within the rapid. Then he hurried downstream to look below Gravedigger Falls. It was near dusk and he could feel the evening darkness lowering itself over the canyon like a shroud.

It was slow going in the rain and storm. The shoreline seemed impenetrable with layer upon layer of brambles and hanging vines. Within 15 minutes, Cruz saw that he was trembling uncontrollably. He stopped near the water's edge to calm himself. Blood dripped from a gash in his forehead. He sat on a low rock and took in deep breaths, then exhaled forcefully. Adrenalin shot through his arms and legs. There was no time to think of fear or death. Only calm. He could almost hear Crawdad's voice: *ease into it; let the river do the work for you.* He stopped fighting the panic and it washed over him, cold and unsettling. He accepted it.

He began to search again. With light fading, he forced himself to mechanically sweep the shallows for any sign of the raft or Crawdad. Thick branches and thorny plants tore at his exposed face and hands. Cactus needles pierced his skin, penetrating the protective raingear like a bayonet tip. At one point he became ensnared in a mass of vines and he thrashed like an animal covered with snakes, lashing out at the night until he broke free and ran blindly through the undergrowth.

He needed help. He knew he could not continue the search alone in the darkness and survive. He watched the sky for signs of clearing, an opening to stars or moon. And when he saw the first glint of constellations, like warm light glowing under a door, his hope soared. He could now see he was out of the main canyon and the steepness of the surrounding walls had lessened. He knew the highway was somewhere above him. He stripped off his lifejacket and raingear, the plastic pants torn and flapping loosely at the knees, and began to climb.

The rock and scree beneath him were loose and unstable. It was as if he were ascending a blanket of sand that was being slowly pulled away. He saw the slope as an endless dune aimed at the heavens and he climbed cautiously, testing each hand or foothold before trusting his weight to it. Imbedded rocks and scrub brush aided his footing as he crisscrossed the face of the canyon wall to avoid cliffs and overhangs. He would set his vision on some shadowy object in the distance, then scramble up until he reached it. Rest. Climb again.

Fear pushed him higher. He knew that if Crawdad had survived somehow and was on the river shoreline below, he would be injured badly and in need of immediate medical treatment. He remembered when the old man had yanked him from the water at Nightmare Corner like some guardian angel and how later he'd said to Cruz, *someday you'll do the same for me.* He would find Crawdad somehow. He would get to him and carry his body to shore so the Kern could not claim it.

He knew there was no stopping now, no going down. His chest heaved like a bellows, each breath searing him as if he were inhaling flame. If he were to stumble or collapse he would surely plummet to his death, too exhausted to catch himself. Occasionally he saw headlights above him, shooting out over the canyon rim, then vanishing. *This is the way it is*, thought Cruz, *this holding on.* He could remember hopping a slow train on a dare when he was a child, and the terror he felt as he dangled from the boxcar, his feet only inches from the sparking wheels. He wondered if Crawdad was clinging to a willow somewhere below, his legs broken, his blood oozing into the river. Cruz felt connected to the old man, as if some invisible line ran from his body to Crawdad's. Each step toward the road lifted his spirit. Each breath. Each second of holding on.

When he reached the highway, he clambered over the guardrail and saw he was on a long straightaway. He looked for road signs but saw none. He sat by the road's edge, his ragged breathing beginning to slow. He could taste blood on his lips and noticed that his knees had been scraped raw, as if he had crawled through shattered glass. He waited for headlights to pierce the night.

He was sitting in a daze when he heard the far-off hum of a car. He limped out onto the road until the glare of high beams illuminated his tattered figure. He raised his weak arms to signal, flapping them like a broken bird, then saw the vehicle slow and pull off. He could hear voices approaching, and he lifted a hand to shield his eyes from the light.

"Shit, this kid's a mess," he heard a stranger say. Then rough hands eased him down into a sitting position against the guardrail.

He saw a truck grind to a halt, then heard the slamming of doors. "Use the radio and get an ambulance," a familiar voice called out. He could see Lou approaching.

"Cruz, are you OK?" he asked, kneeling beside him.

"I'm fine," Cruz answered, "but Lou . . ." he

reached out and gripped his arm, "... it's Crawdad. He's still down there. We flipped and I got thrown out. Crawdad stayed with the boat and went over Gravedigger Falls. I couldn't get to him."

"Relax," said Lou. "We'll find him. You're in no shape to go searching for his body."

"But maybe he's not dead, maybe he made it through."

"Maybe so," said Lou. "If anybody could make it through the falls, it'd be Crawdad. Now we gotta get you to the hospital."

Cruz closed his eyes. Minutes passed. He felt as if he were floating in a cloud of mist, his body supported only by air, the movements around him far away. He smelled the pungent odor of antiseptic from the first-aid kit. He heard the rip of paper as rolls of sterile gauze were torn open, and in the distance, the shrill, penetrating sound of a siren approaching.

When he opened his eyes he saw Walker standing in front of him. He was staring down as if he were gazing at a wounded animal found by the roadside. Lou was over by the truck. A crowd of men huddled around him as he talked with headquarters on the radio.

"He almost killed you," Walker said, "him and all his river gods. I tried to warn you. He had no respect for the power of the Kern. None. Never did. That's what killed him."

"Why aren't you out looking for him?" asked Cruz. "He might still be alive down there. He could be dying."

"Because I respect the river," said Walker. "I've got more sense than to go out searching for a dead man in the middle of the night when the Kern's running sky high."

Something snapped inside Cruz. At first, he felt nothing, no pain or anger or exhaustion. He noticed a rip in the left knee of Walker's jeans. A stranger smoked a cigarette nearby, its red tip gleaming like a firefly in the darkness. Then a wave of heat, perilous and unchanging, rolled through him. He wanted to kill Walker, crush his skull like pulp on the asphalt. He wanted to scream and hear his own voice shatter the stillness. He wanted to hit him with his fists in the ribs, shoulder, face, until teeth cut into his knuckles. But he waited.

"These things happen," Walker said. "People die in this line of work."

Lou came and led him to the ambulance, helped him inside where he could lie down on a stretcher. Cruz knew it would be days before he could cry, when the loneliness would grip him and he would be haunted by Crawdad. He knew that pain in his life was something to guard against, a scorpion hidden in the dust. Yet he felt it, deep and stinging, as if the past had never existed. He held on to what he had left. The beautiful face of a dead woman. A prayer from an old man. *May the river gods be with us*, he thought.

And Brother Blue.

SECOND DESCENT

By Franz Lidz

Second expeditions are often like losing a close decision in a heavyweight title fight; you've been in the same ring, you've taken a lot of punches, but all you get is a footnote in a record book. Everyone knows that Robert Peary led the first successful assault on the North Pole, and that Sir Edmund Hillary's party made the initial ascent of Everest, but who was second? Robert Scott, who lost the race to be the first to reach the South Pole, had to freeze to death to be remembered.

The maiden voyage on Africa's Zambezi River in October 1981 wasn't exactly on the order of Amundsen's navigation of the Northwest Passage or even John Smith's sail up the Chesapeake, but still *National Geographic* was there to photograph it, Pan Am underwrote it, and Kenneth Kaunda, the founding father of Zambia, celebrated it with banquets, testimonials, and tribal dances. The Zambezi marks the border between Zambia and Zimbabwe. Across the water, Zimbabwe provided army helicopters for aerial scouting and emergency evacuations. ABC sent a camera crew to document the occasion for its "American Sportsman" show and even enlisted LeVar Burton, who played young Kunta Kinte in "Roots," to ride along. The film clips that ran showed grizzled and dangerous adventure: an inflatable raft upended by 15-foot waves, a crocodile launching itself into the water; a rugged and primitive struggle with the unknown.

In truth, the first trip had more support than the Entebbe raid. According to several members of the expedition, the ABC hype included footage of a crocodile that was actually penned at a local crocodile ranch; Burton and the camera crew were flown out of the wilds every night to a posh resort hotel, and the raft capsized only after a producer offered $100 to the first boatman who flipped his boat on camera.

The second descent, late in the summer of 1982, marked the opening of regular commercial runs down the Zambezi. It had less fanfare than its predecessor and covered the same territory, but was perhaps a little more difficult. This modest week-long expedition featured only the rag-

"Rich's to Rags," the first rapid on the Zambezi below Victoria Falls, named after Richard Bangs, one of the leaders of the first Zambezi expedition. Photo by Bart Henderson/SOBEK.

Victoria Falls, starting point on the Zambezi, is twice as high as Niagara. Photo by John Kramer/SOBEK.

ing river and, for celebrities, a periodontist from Providence, Rhode Island. Our three-raft party of four boatmen, a local guide and eight passengers put in at the Boiling Point, a whirlpool rapid near the base of mile-wide Victoria Falls. The boatmen were veterans of the world's great rafting rivers: Turkey's Coruh, Chile's Bio-Bio and North America's preeminent whitewater adventure, the Colorado. But the Zambezi was perhaps an even greater challenge: more than half a dozen of its rapids are steeper and swifter than the Colorado's legendary Lava Falls. Some of the rapids

have such precipitous drops that they're waterfalls. The only way to get around them is to portage.

From the Boiling Point we watch the Zambezi cascading in sheer columns twice as high as Niagara Falls. The Kololo tribe, which invaded the area from the south in 1838, called the falls Masi-O-Tunya, the smoke that thunders. David Livingstone, the Scottish explorer/missionary who arrived on the scene 17 years later, wrote in a moment of uncharacteristic lyricism: "The snow-white sheet seemed like myriads of small

A raft lurches into one of those fabled Zambezi rapids that tend to swallow rafts and spit them out half-digested. Photo by Franz Lidz.

comets rushing on in one direction, each of which left behind its nucleus rays of foam.'' The optimistic Livingstone was confident that British rectitude and ingenuity would find a way for his steamships to navigate the Zambezi, waterfalls and all. He spent most of his adult life exploring the route. But Livingstone died before anyone negotiated the Zambezi on a log, much less a steamboat.

Indeed, as a raft on the first voyage careered through one rapid, a villager watched from the shore in slack-jawed awe. ''I could not believe my eyes,'' he told members of the party later. ''That eddy is called Mahombero, and when

fishermen upstream fall into the rapids, their bodies always wash up there. No one has every survived those rapids.''

We shoot through the salt-streaked basalt cliffs of Batako Gorge, and down a series of stomach-wrenching rapids. On the Colorado, the rapids all have histories and evocative names: Upset, Tuna Creek, Sockdolager. Here, the territory is pretty much uncharted, and the rapids have numbers, not names. After 11, the first expedition stopped counting.

By midafternoon we reach a hydroelectric power station at the head of number five, a humongous rapid boiling with holes. At this

Soirée on the Zambian side of the river, where the land mines are fewer. Photo by Franz Lidz.

point on the previous trip, Burton and prominent river historian Grant Rogers were tossed from their raft into the swirling current. Rogers cracked several ribs and had to be helicoptered to a hospital.

Two of our boatmen elect to line their rafts around the rapid. The third decides to run it, and I decide to go along. A troupe of baboons on the Zambian side barks at us. They seem to be laughing. No baboon ever tried to run the Zambezi.

Weighted down with seven volunteers, the boat rides the crest of a massive wave, punches through a wall of water, gets slapped over the plume of another wave, but veers too close to a

gaping hole. The raft folds over in the hole. I go down in the greenish-white water for what seems like a week, but is really a few seconds. I bob to the surface thinking the boat must be 80 feet in front of me, but actually it's within reach. As I hoist myself onto the overturned raft, I start to wonder if the baboons were right.

Farther downstream we float past the patchy scrub of the river corridor. Rows of spindly mopane trees on the canyon's rim overlook our descent like Bantu sentinels. Fish eagles and white-fronted bee-eaters wheel about overhead. Herds of small antelopes called duikers scurry up the rocky brown slopes. The hills are dotted

A rare calm stretch. To discourage crocodiles from biting the rafts, passengers are equipped with baseball-sized stones they call "croc rocks." Photo by Ian Murphy/SOBEK.

with trees: the mukwena, muzwili, and mubako, and the baobab (the last believed to be enchanted because it looks as if it's been planted upside down). The Portuguese explorer Manuel Barreto, who made the first recorded sighting of the middle Zambezi in 1667, wrote that the river flowed through a land, "where only birds can fly or serpents crawl."

The fare Barreto ate was far more modest than the sort of Southern California cuisine we were served: avocados, oranges, cheese, charbroiled steaks, and peanut butter. The boatmen cook. We wash up in the river, and take our baths there.

We sleep in sleeping bags in pup tents. Toilet functions are performed in the bush and on the banks of the river.

On the third night we camp on a scarp of squeaky white sand on the Zimbabwe side. The Zimbabwe shore is less desirable because it was mined extensively during the war for independence. Nobody is quite sure if any live mines remain, though it's believed that most were either washed away or triggered by baboons.

We walk very lightly.

As I leave the evening campfire, I come upon a trail of large animal tracks.

"Are these leopard prints?" I ask Enock, our Lozi guide.

"There are no leopards here," he says.

"No leopards anywhere on the Zambezi?"

"No leopards."

"Then what kind of tracks are they?"

"Leopard."

We sleep very lightly, too.

The following day we reach a couple of unnavigable 20-foot waterfalls. This is what really stopped Livingstone. A dam is planned at the first that may someday submerge most of the major rapids under a reservoir.

The afternoon is spent portaging the rafts over the jagged cliffs. The heat is intense. We fortify ourselves with Sobel's Kentucky Cookies, a crumbly Zimbabwe confection.

"Flatdogs!" our boatman shouts on the fifth day. That's explorer talk for crocodiles. Though there aren't as many crocodiles in Africa as there used to be, they still kill about three people a day, and one a week in Zambia. We pass within several yards of an eight-footer lazing on a smooth ledge. It leers, then slides into the water and follows our boat. Enock claims crocodiles think inflatable rafts are dead hippos.

To discourage crocodiles from biting the rafts we came equipped with baseball-sized stones that are referred to as "croc rocks." The crocodile steams toward us with only its eyes and nostrils visible, like a half-submerged submarine. I unload my best sinker, but miss the strike zone. Apparently, I came close enough. The crocodile crash-dives, pops up again a minute later, rolls over and drifts off.

The rest of the trip seems almost anticlimactic. We sight dozens of crocodiles and hippos, but none venture close to the rafts. The Zambezi has slowed considerably.

We come to a stretch where the river is cut by immense black boulders, as smooth as Lipchitz sculptures. We veer right where the first expedition veered left and wind up smack in the middle of a horror of a rapid. The raft turns on its side like a lazy hippo. A camera flips out of the raft, and so do I. My dunking seems more serious though. Crocodiles don't eat cameras.

On the final day we cruise past a village of thatched huts, the first sign of civilization in days. Ragged-clothed men with switches are fishing for bream and tiger fish. We expect to be treated like great explorers, but instead the fishermen try to sell us bream at $5 apiece, the tourist price! Second expeditions don't get any respect.

DAREDEVIL AL FAUSSETT

By Whit Deschner

Sunset Falls on Washington's Skykomish River drops 104 feet over a 275-foot granite slide. Many a boater has stood spellbound alongside the roaring explosion of waters and inevitably asked, "Can it be run?" The answer is a fat ho hum to those who believe they can push the modern limits of white-water boating: It was run in 1926. The man's name was Al Faussett.

And Sunset Falls was only the beginning of Faussett's cataract-jumping career. Over a period of four years, he descended six of the Northwest's most treacherous falls—including 212-foot Shoshone, 47 feet higher than Niagara!

Up until 1926 Faussett had been a lumberjack or, as they were known back then, a "dirtyneck." He ran a gyppo operation trying to compete against Weyerhaeuser. Faussett might have kept on running his shoestring logging outfit had it not been for Fox Studios, which was in the area to shoot a western.

The script for Fox's soundless feature called for an Indian to ride over a falls in a dugout. Their choice for the take was Sunset and they offered $1,500 to anyone who would jump the falls.

Faussett was the lone taker of the bait. However, when he saw Fox's canoe he claimed it was far from adequate for such a feat. He would craft his own. Faussett felled a spruce and hand-hewed from it a 34-foot canoe.

But when Faussett added safety features to his canoe there was little resemblance to an Indian dugout. He had cowled the foredeck over with sheet metal, the aft deck with canvas. In the stern he left a small opening where he would strap

Sunset Falls was probably Faussett's most spectacular ride. Photo courtesy Lee Pickett.

**Faussett gliding into calm water after running Sunset Falls in 1926. His life
jacket was an inner tube wrapped around his body. Photo courtesy Lee Pickett.**

himself in. To absorb the impact of colliding with boulders Faussett fastened to the hull five-foot lengths of vine maple at various angles. When Fox saw the finished boat they reneged on their offer.

Faussett wasn't going to collect his $1,500 but his friends convinced him that that was no reason why his canoe should start gathering termites. Thus it was announced that on May 30, 1926, Al Faussett would run Sunset Falls. A dollar admission would be charged.

Whether or not the enterpriser knew what he was in for, he spoke confidently of the ride, telling the *Everett News*, "It will be a dangerous and thrilling ride. But the people who come will see me make a cool ride, and one they had never anticipated. There is nothing to be afraid of, for I have studied the dangers carefully and believe I can negotiate these falls where 20 men have lost their lives."

On May 30, a crowd of 3,000 gathered along the banks in the cool mist of the falls. It was not an event to be missed. Some had come the night before and a good share had crashed the gate. The event was to have taken place at one o'clock. It was now four and the crowd was growing impatient. At last word rushed through the crowd that Faussett was adrift in his canoe, floating to the brink.

At a speed of 80 m.p.h. the canoe crashed through the falls engulfed in tons of pounding water. The boat grazed over a large granite protrusion and shot almost clear of the water only to slam back down and disappear. It was several sec-

Faussett and his Eagle Falls boat. Photo courtesy Lee Pickett.

onds before the boat and its human cargo reappeared, emerging out of the spray and gliding free into the pool below. When Fausett waved to the crowd they erupted, clapping and cheering.

In the *Everett News* Faussett wrote of his descent, "People will never know and little did I dream of the power of those treacherous waters in the falls. When I went under, the water hit me with a crushing force and hurt my lungs. It twisted my body and head. I was hurt inside and could not breathe. The water came so fast it crammed down my nostrils and throat.

"At no time was I afraid of those falls, not even when the water seemed to be crushing the very life out of me. It was all over in a few seconds, and when I saw the light of day as I rode out of the turbulent waters, I thanked God that I had

ridden safely through. I have challenged the world to the effect that I can ride anywhere any human can in my good canoe."

As Irv, Al Faussett's son, said of his father, "Dad was another Evel Knievel. He was just born 40 years too soon. There just wasn't the instant publicity back then to make him rich and famous."

Three months later and four miles upstream from Sunset, Faussett chose to run Eagle Falls, a series of jagged tiers dropping a total of 40 feet. This time the daredevil concluded his longevity might be increased if he rode inside of the boat. For his new craft he hollowed out two halves of a log and banded them together. It was 16 feet long, cigar-shaped and had a trap door for access.

Due to low water the Labor Day event was more

Faussett trapped in Eagle Falls. Photo courtesy Lee Pickett.

comical than spectacular. Faussett was bid good luck by his friends, climbed in his boat, shut the hatch, and was shoved into the lazy current.

Halfway through the falls the boat wedged in the rocks. Faussett opened the hatch, yelling for assistance. His friends managed to knock the boat loose with a pike pole, and it and Faussett bounced to the bottom of the falls without mishap.

"On to Snoqualmie and Niagara," he told the press.

Irv said of his father, "In those days people back East thought of Washington and Oregon as still territories. What people did in the Northwest didn't matter to others. Dad wanted to go east and do Niagara. He wanted to put Washington on the map."

Since Niagara was too far away, Faussett announced he would run 216-foot Snoqualmie Falls. But Puget Power, which owned the land adjoining the falls, refused to let the adventurer run, for fear of a lawsuit.

Faussett resolved to run one of the obscure falls upstream from Snoqualmie but he was foiled again, this time by the King County sheriff, who figured he was saving Faussett's life by stopping him.

The next year Faussett announced he would go elsewhere to run his waterfalls. He went to Spokane to run Spokane Falls. The city officials were not sure whose jurisdiction it was to stop Faussett. The buck was passed to the chief of police, who concluded that it was Faussett's decision whether or not he wanted to kill himself.

However, Faussett was not allowed to charge admission.

On June 3, 1927, more than half of Spokane's population crammed along the banks to watch Faussett get swept over the falls. As Faussett climbed in his 775-pound boat, similar to the one used in Eagle, the crowd crammed closer.

Then the river rushed the craft into the 75-foot staircase cataract—a torrent of awesome power. The boat dropped over the first step, somersaulting in the uproar. It then floated free only to be sucked into a whirlpool, tossed like confetti in a tornado. There it remained spinning around for over 20 minutes until it finally swept close enough to shore to allow several men to pull it to safety. Faussett staggered from the boat with blood dripping down his face and was hurried into an ambulance.

"They've got whiskers on 'em (the falls) an' they sure can give a feller an awful tossing," he told the *Spokesman Review*. He had received a slight concussion along with numerous cuts and bruises. Several hours later the boat worked free of its moorings and went over the lower section of the falls, where it was smashed into pieces and never seen again. Faussett quit for the season. One bump on the head was enough.

But next year he was back, this time in Oregon, to jump 40-foot Oregon City Falls. Faussett's new boat was 30 feet long. His plan was to paddle up to the falls, align the boat bow first, duck inside and close the hatch.

It was the last day of March. A crowd of 10,000 was on hand and as Faussett and boat reached the brink the crowd was aware that something was drastically wrong. Faussett fought to line the boat up but gusting winds and a powerful current spun the boat sideways. And that's how it went over. Faussett had failed to get the hatch closed. The boat landed upside down, then disappeared into the froth for over a minute before coming into view.

In the swift current below the falls it took the rescue team six minutes to reach the boat. When they finally righted it, a wet and smiling Faussett emerged.

When the *Oregonian* asked Faussett about the ride he replied, "The canoe is the finest craft on the water. Without it I couldn't have made it. We hit the middle of the falls just right, but the strong wind and current simply made me powerless to shoot the rapids as I had planned. I had no time to close the trap door above me so I just hung on. Air under the upturned boat made it possible for me to breathe.

"Going through those rapids sounded like a million cowbells to me. You can't imagine the queer sensation of it. How many times the boat turned over I don't know. About twice, I thought, but others said many times. What I do when I'm buried in water like that I'm not accountable for. I simply hang on. What else is there to do?"

The daredevil's next exploit was to shoot the 186-foot Silver Creek Falls. However, the group of businessmen who owned the property surrounding the falls refused to let Faussett carry out his plans. In order to run the drop, Faussett first had to buy it along with the adjoining 100 acres.

On July 1, 5,000 people crowded into the area to watch the plunge. Dirt roads were jammed with Model Ts. Some of the people never made it to the event because the traffic was so bad.

Faussett's new boat looked like an obese rugby ball. It was made with a wooden skeleton, filled with 36 car innertubes, and covered with orange canvas. It weighed 180 pounds. In order to avoid bouncing off the rock ledge on the way down, Faussett built a ramp protruding 12 feet out past the brink.

Faussett and his boat arched 186 feet into the pool below. Unfortunately, the boat belly flopped instead of landing nose first as planned.

"There wasn't a scared bone in his body," Irv said. But when he crashed into the pool below there were several broken ones; a few ribs, one wrist, both ankles were sprained and he couldn't move his bowels for four days.

Faussett still wanted to run Niagara but the logistics of getting there with a boat were too complicated. So Faussett announced he would run Shoshone Falls on the Snake River in Idaho. It was 212 feet high—47 feet higher than Niagara.

The date was July 28, 1929 and the water conditions on the Snake were low. To make the ride feasible the Idaho Power Company resolved to open the gates of a diversion dam upstream half an hour before the ride.

Again Faussett used the canvas boat that he had used on Silver Creek. The crowd of 5,000 would be warned with a series of bombs that he was ready to leap—four at 15 minutes, three at 10 minutes and two at 5 minutes before the stunt. One bomb would give alarm that Faussett was floating to the brink. A salvo of bombs were to be fired indicating that Faussett was injured and on his way to the hospital.

To deflect the boat from rock jutting out in the middle of the falls a wire was attached upstream to a large boulder, then threaded through a three-inch diameter ring on the boat. The other end of the wire would be held below by one of the rescue team.

After making adjustments on his boat, Faussett was ready. A single bomb was fired as he was set adrift in the river. Unfortunately the water released from the dam didn't give the boat enough draw and twice it hung up on the bottom, the last time right on the brink. Two men waded out to the boat and gave it a shove over the falls.

He dropped 212 feet—the highest falls ever jumped.

Faussett emerged from his boat with only a broken right hand. A salvo of bombs were fired off. For the event Faussett received $733.

The extra 47 feet didn't mean much to the daredevil though. "Dad still wanted to run Niagara. It was the falls that had a name to it. Things didn't work out and he never got back there. Even when Dad was in his sixties (25 years later) he still had plans for Niagara."

In February 1948, the man who once described himself as "feeling more at home in a logging camp than in a crowd" "went west." He died of cancer.

"That's not what really killed him," Irv said. "He couldn't stand the regimentation of being in a rest home. It was the first time in his life someone told him what to do: when to turn off the light, when to go to bed. It got him down and he just couldn't take it."

A segment of the obituary in a Seattle newspaper read: "If there are any rivers where Al Faussett is now, he'll be hunting for a waterfall over which to leap."

Irv said of his father, "He lived three lives to most men's one. He got a lot of fun out of life. Funny thing was he never knew how to swim."

RAFTING WITH THE BBC

By David Roberts

I was reading a book in the hotel bar when a red-haired man wearing shorts and a lifejacket walked in. He looked wet. It took me a moment to recognize him as the BBC assistant cameraman, whom I had met the day before.

I said, "Hi. How's it going?"

He stared back wildly. "Haven't you heard? The others are all dead. I'm the only one left."

This was, to put it blandly, an inauspicious way to begin an expedition.

It was August 1983. We had gathered in Kundiawa, a little town in the highlands of Papua New Guinea, to attempt the first descent of some significant portion of the Wahgi-Tua-Purari, one of Southeast Asia's great wilderness rivers. "We" were an odd-shaped group of 17, the core of which was seven old hands from an adventure-travel company whose collective notion of the purpose of existence had much to do with riding rafts down rapids nobody else had ever dared to navigate. Photographer Nick Nichols and I were aboard because we had convinced *GEO* magazine that there was a story in this. Eighteen-year-

old apprentice guide Renée Goddard had been invited because another magazine, sponsored by the Army and aimed at 18-year-olds, was eager to chronicle the adventure if it happened to involve an authentic 18-year-old.

Then there was the BBC. The moguls of British television had decided to follow up their popular series "Great Railway Journeys" with a similar batch of films about rivers. Most were to be on tame waterways like the Nile and the Mekong, but they wanted to throw in one "adventure" river, and our assault on the Wahgi-Tua-Purari had gotten the nod. On location in New Guinea, there was a director, a chief cameraman and his assistant, an American cameraman on loan, a soundman, a troubleshooter, and the show's "personality"—a photogenic adventurer through whose cinematic derring-do the story would be told.

The person who had put together this remarkable package (for once, the jargon of advertising supplies the most apt word) was Richard Bangs, co-founder and president of Sobek. Bangs is a rafting wild man of hoary pedigree, who has done

**In search of a river. But the boxes were empty and much of
the hauling was for show. Photo by John Kramer/SOBEK.**

his time in the Stygian keepers and hydraulics of
the world's roughest rivers. He is also a formida-
bly seductive entrepreneur, the kind of person
who needs only a few beers and a sketch on the
back of an envelope to talk you into changing
your life. In the service of his powers of persua-
sion, he has been known to reassure a bit blithely,
to estimate a bit grandly. "Bangsian Hype" is a
term in local usage in Angels Camp, California,
where Sobek is quartered.

In 1977 Bangs and a few cronies had come to
New Guinea and run the Watut and Yuat rivers,
the latter at nearly the cost of their lives. Un-
abashed, Bangs had longed ever since to try the
Wahgi, which flows more than 400 miles from

Mount Hagen south through a series of remote
and awesome canyons, changing its name first to
the Tua, then to the Purari, before spilling into
the Gulf of Papua. Because of the difficulty of
access, the trip would be an expensive one, and
there was no hope of recovering the investment
by turning it into a commercial float trip. It would
be a one-shot expedition. The project thus
needed BBC money, and the attention of *GEO*
magazine (not to mention a magazine about
18-year-olds) would not hurt.

I had met Richard the year before and hit it off
with him from the start. Our budding friendship
had convinced me that the Wahgi venture was
suitable for a person of my capabilities. Yet as

the trip approached, I began to feel apprehension. Some of it was occasioned by the fact that I have never learned to swim—this despite the helpful efforts of playmates all the way through junior high school who would push me into the deep end of the swimming pool or hold me underwater in the shallow end. "Don't worry, Dave," Richard had said over a beer, "anything you don't like the looks of, you can walk around." Without yet knowing its name, I had sniffed the scent of Bangsian Hype.

I was enthusiastic about New Guinea, eager to plunge into its wilderness. But the Wahgi was clearly a serious proposition, and as the expedition loomed in my future, my malaise focused on the issue of motivation. The descent of the river was no obsession of mine. That belonged to guides like Richard. Was even the best writing assignment worth risking my life on the Wahgi? Privately I welcomed the BBC to the project, as a distraction from the monomania of getting downstream at all costs, as a leavening of sheer amateurism to make my own ineptness less conspicuous.

During the first days in New Guinea, I began to relax. The logistical thickets were so dense it seemed we might never fight our way through to the riverbank. From the start, it was clear that Richard and the BBC director, Clive Syddall, were at serious cross-purposes. Clive seemed gentle and intelligent, quick to laugh. He told me that he had taught economics at Oxford. But he was not an outdoorsman, and he was plainly nervous about the jungle. Moreover, he seemed indeci-

sive; it took him forever to decide on each day's course of action.

The Sobek guides were basically interested in running the river; Clive wanted to make a good movie. The BBC was footing the bill, so Richard patiently humored the director, hoping to maneuver him into agreeing to as much "real" river as we could buy. The two men compromised on the Tua, the continuously turgid middle section of the system, about 100 miles long. We would have to helicopter in and out.

Unfortunately, Clive's ideas about what backwoods New Guinea should look like owed less to geographical reality than to other movies—in particular *Raiders of the Lost Ark*, to which he made frequent and devout reference. In the first few days, we had some highland natives dress up in war paint and carry empty metal boxes slung from boat oars up a hillside, while being filmed in silhouette against the sunset. This served to record Sobek's search for the "put-in" on the Tua. We paid another gang of locals to stage a Sing-Sing, or traditional dance-feast ceremony. On a platform woven from green bamboo, we explorers sat like after-dinner speakers. At the climactic moment, a ribbon strung between two Sobek oars was snipped by a local politico. The Sing-Sing was brilliant and exuberant, but we had only the vaguest notion as to what it signified (something to do with pigs: pig-killing? pig-acquiring?). In the middle of the show, I realized that we didn't even know the name of the tribe we were watching.

There was a major problem looming. The BBC was reluctant to put its expensive cameras in the

Papua New Guinea belongs to the locals, but the BBC meant to capture some of its whitewater for television. Photo by Richard Bangs/SOBEK.

boats, and they had little or no rafting experience. Clive had hired veteran American whitewater cinematographer Roger Brown, who had no such compunctions, to shoot with his own cameras from on board.

As a shakedown, a bunch of us did a 12-mile float on the Wahgi near Kundiawa, putting in and taking out from road bridges. The half-day trip turned into pure idyll, as we glided among green hills, through a limestone gorge, past hidden waterfalls. The only two real rapids were easily scouted and run. It was the perfect opportunity to lay to rest BBC anxiety, and Richard persuaded Clive and crew to duplicate the trip the next day —without cameras.

It rained heavily all night, and the river was a full four feet higher than it had been the previous day, but two rafts set out in midmorning. At the first rapid, the current was too powerful for the boats to pull to shore, and one raft plunged into the worst part of the "hole." It did not flip, but rather bounced crazily in place, trapped by the hole as river water poured into it from above. One by one the passengers were jounced loose and into the current.

Taking a "swim" is old hat for river runners, but a terrifying experience for a novice. Two of the refugees, including Clive himself, were hauled to safety a little ways downstream by the other boat, and the other two—assistant cameraman Alan Smith and head cameraman Mike Spooner —eddied out near shore, one on each bank. Had they sat tight and waited, the captains would have walked back upstream shortly to gather them up. But Smith and Spooner were, quite independently, seized with the same impulse—to flee through the jungle.

Smith had come to rest on the left, or Kundiawa, side of the Wahgi, and he had a relatively brief ordeal. Natives found him and helped him to the road, where he got a ride to town from a clergyman. But as he stumbled into the hotel bar and found me, Smith believed quite sincerely that he was the only survivor of an appalling tragedy.

The rest of us immediately set out to determine what had happened. We joined Richard, who had already been waiting for hours at the take-out. Just before dusk, the boats appeared. To our dismay, Spooner was still missing. With a grim sense of futility, several parties set out after dark in the rain to attempt a rescue. On the right side of the Wahgi, where Spooner had last been seen crawling to shore, there was only jungle, scattered native huts, and—21 miles away by a tortuous dirt road—the Catholic mission of Neragaima.

The group I was with took a Jeep up to the mission. With darkness a dense fog had set in, and the wet road became almost as slick as ice. On hairpin bends the headlights bounced blindly off fog, intimating the precipice about a foot away. It was the most frightening backcountry drive I have ever been on, but the natives who drove the Jeep seemed to treat it as good sport.

Shortly before midnight we got to Neragaima where, to our astonishment and relief, we found Spooner abed. George Fuller, our doctor, was the only person allowed to visit him. Spooner, George revealed, had suffered a punctured eardrum and a possible skull fracture. Despite losing one shoe, he had walked, with native assistance, some six miles through the bush to Neragaima. A nurse told us that she had found Spooner sitting on the grass. "I went up and said, 'Hullo.' He answered, 'Hullo, I'm from the BBC.' I was looking around for the cameras, but then he simply burst into tears."

Spooner was furious with Sobek and refused even to talk to Richard. Back in Kundiawa he remained bedridden, and he was clearly out of commission for the rest of the trip. After several days he told me his story. He had had an eerie premonition about the whole New Guinea trip, and in Port Moresby had left a letter for his wife. As the flooding river had knocked him out of the boat, he had instantly remembered the letter. He was tossed around underwater "like in a washing machine." He pictured his wife and his three-year-old daughter and thought, "This is it. This is how I die."

Spooner felt his shoe come off in the water, and thought that a crocodile was nibbling at his foot. When he eddied out and crawled on shore, his only impulse was to put as much distance between himself and the river as he could. He took a stick and beat the ground in front of him to clear out any snakes. After a while he ran into a man in a loincloth. Spooner's mind filled with thoughts of headhunters. But the stranger seemed anxious to help. "I made the noise of a car and tried to indicate the main road. The man gave me a 'We go' signal."

A series of villagers led Spooner, with one bare foot, bleeding from the ear, and probably in shock, all the way to Neragaima. "They were all very nice," he said. "It poured rain at one point, and some natives cut banana leaves for an umbrella for me. I gave one old chap my compass that I carry everywhere. He put it on top of his head and thought it was wonderful." At a hut in the bushes a native supplied Spooner with a bottle of Cherry-Ade and some American biscuits.

"I was in Jamaica during an assassination attempt, right in the middle of the gunfire," Spooner told me. "That wasn't so bad. At least you knew where you could go. In the river I couldn't do anything. There's no way I'm ever going to get in a blasted boat again."

During the next few days, the expedition itself was in jeopardy, and tensions were high. Both cameramen joined Clive in blaming Sobek for not briefing them adequately before the Wahgi fiasco. The Sobek guides swore that nobody in their collective experience had ever bolted after washing ashore. For the first time a clear split—Sobek vs. the BBC—became manifest. It was a division that would dog the whole expedition.

Nevertheless, on August 22 both the BBC and Sobek were helicoptered in to an ample gravel bar near the head of the Tua. We were no longer in the genial highlands. I stepped out of the chopper into the iron heat of the jungle: cicadas whining in the treetops, black rocks too hot to walk on, a mud-colored maelstrom of river seething through the claustrophobic wedge of the valley. Yet within an hour I had begun to love the place. I couldn't wait to get into a raft.

The BBC had hired a woman named Christina Dodwell to be the film's star. Christina had spent a number of years touring the New Guinea wilderness, mostly alone, and had just published a book detailing her extraordinary adventures. A week into the trip, however, she remained something of an enigma. She was a tall, slender woman, perhaps in her early thirties, with long, straight blond hair. Most of the time she wore a green Aussie-style bush hat set at a rakish angle. As the other writer in the neighborhood, I had tried two or three times to strike up a conversation, but Christina had not encouraged shoptalk. Having dug up a copy of her book, I had brought it along to read on the Tua.

I was surprised to notice at our first camp that Christina couldn't figure out how to set up her tent. She admitted, in fact, that she had never before slept in a tent. Always before she had just thrown up a hammock or laid out her duffel on the ground. Several men from Sobek obligingly helped her erect her shelter.

The Wahgi shakedown had been designed to convince Clive and company that it was not unthinkable to ride in the boats with us. Such ambitions were by now, of course, phantasmal. Still, we hoped that Clive's first night of camping with the gang would infect him with the spirit of the trip, and indeed, at breakfast on the second day he seemed quite pleased with the whole enterprise. He had come up with a pith helmet, which he was to wear constantly during the next week. But it turned out that that was the last time the BBC crew stayed overnight. Roger Brown chose to camp out with us, as did Christina. But from then on the BBC commuted daily by helicopter to and from the hotel in Kundiawa.

On the second day, all the guides were itching to get onto the river, and the camp was hopping at 6 A.M. But Clive needed to think out the day's shooting, and we did not push off until just before noon. We spent three and a half hours filming an exciting rapid, one that I was very happy to walk around. But by late afternoon, despite a surge of adrenalin every time a wave splashed me, I was starting to get the hang of this daredevil sport. My role in the boat was a simple one, which captain Mike Boyle had explained succinctly: "Shut up and hang on."

Just as I was thinking that river running might be fun, Skip Horner's boat flipped. Mike's raft took up the chase. We hauled two of the castaways aboard; the other two rode through another bad rapid clinging to their upside-down craft. At last Boyle towed eight people and two boats to the blessed firmness of shore—just where we had planned to camp. In the middle of this drama, we had become aware of the helicopter screaming over our heads; even though we cursed its noise and the wind its rotors blasted us with, we hoped Clive was getting his footage. As soon as we touched the shore, everybody cheered with relief.

The helicopter landed; Richard disappeared with Clive in a story conference. Later we learned that the director had decided that on the morrow we should heli-lift the boats back upstream and run through the thing again. Incredulity gave way to obscenity—though the guides kept their derision from Clive's ears.

In the morning the BBC was an hour and a half late for our rendezvous. We sat and stewed in our boats; it was a gorgeous day, and the river ached to be run. Once the helicopter arrived, it took Clive another two hours to decide what to do. During the wait, the soundman revealed to me that they had been slow getting off from Kundiawa because of a hassle in changing rooms in their hotel.

It was Richard's birthday, and that night his cronies baked a surprise cake over the campfire and hauled out four bottles of Australian cabernet. Richard regaled us with a conversation he had had with Clive. "I hope you don't have wine in your supplies," the director had said. "No wine," Richard had averred. "Because," continued Clive, "the weight is really getting out of hand." Richard looked battle-fatigued. Clive, he said, had threatened that morning to abort the whole project if they didn't haul the boats back upstream and again run the rapid where Skip's boat had flipped. Richard had called his bluff.

That day we were stopped cold a little after

In the Decadent Age of Exploration, helicopters often steal the show, in more ways than one. Photo by John Kramer/SOBEK.

noon. A major rapid turned out to stretch, uninterrupted, for half a mile. The jungle was so thick it took two hours just to scout the rapid. By nightfall we were camped in drizzling rain in miserable semi-bivouacs among a mass of boulders. Christina had flown back to Kundiawa with the BBC. She told Renée she wasn't feeling well. The absence of the BBC induced a friendly intimacy in our uncomfortable camp: We could poke fun at Clive to our heart's content.

The guides had been mulling over the nasty rapid in their minds. Skip pointed out that it wasn't the individual "moves" that made it so tough; it was the lack of calm water between them in which to recover. On Sobek's descent of the

Indus a few years before, John Kramer had run a similar rapid after the whole group had portaged it. Now a certain gleam came into his eye as he stared at the Tua. But he backed down. "You'd run it if it were the only way out of here," John said. "But it's a life-or-death proposition, not a sporting one."

The portage, thanks to the fiendish vegetation, would take at least two days, the guides insisted. Guiltily, they reconciled themselves to the alternative. The helicopter, which we had cursed only yesterday—the symbol of the artificiality that the BBC was forcing upon us—could be used to lift all our gear and boats past the half-mile rapid. The next morning, the heli-lift went like clockwork. Park, our crack Korean pilot, got everything downstream in only two hours.

By that night morale had plunged to a new low. Clive wanted to boat one more day and pull out, less than halfway down the Tua. He had told Richard, "You can go on down if you want, but you'll have to get yourselves out." Before he had flown back to his hotel, he had filmed Christina getting in and out of the chopper and perusing the map with Skip. For the film, she asked him questions like, "Where are we, Skip?" and "Are there rapids?"

I had been reading her book. In it, she recounted paddling a dugout canoe by herself the length of the Sepik River, riding a horse for a thousand miles through the highlands, and walking for two weeks from Oksapmin to Kopiago, passing through the notorious "broken-bottle country." I had just read an account of one of the earliest jaunts through this jagged, waterless karst terrain, by the famed explorer Jack Hides. Hides had written that many of his porters had been "disabled by deep gashes caused by the limestone . . . It tore our boots to pieces, and whenever we slipped it did likewise with our bodies."

Christina, however, claimed to have walked across the broken-bottle country *barefoot*, having forgotten to bring boots. I had begun to wonder about the book, and about her. She had described her ascent of Mount Wilhelm, the country's highest peak, and had spoken of gazing at Lakes Pinde and Aunde from the summit. I had been up Mount Wilhelm myself just a week before the trip and knew the lakes could not be seen from the top. Christina's apparent ineptitude around camp, moreover, extended beyond not knowing how to set up her tent. She was the only person who generally avoided helping with the chores. Instead, she spent much of her time brushing her hair, writing in her notebook, and rolling cigarettes.

I began to seek her out, asking her "innocent" questions; and she, no doubt understandably, began to avoid me. Yet to my face she claimed the most astounding things—to have ridden her horse to 16,000 feet on Mount Kenya in Africa, for instance, or to have ridden as much as 60 miles a day in the New Guinea highlands without benefit of roads or trails. At one point she asked me what books I had written. I told her my latest had been called *Great Exploration Hoaxes*. She looked at me coolly and said, "Did you find any hoaxes in New Guinea?" I said no. "Because," she said, "there are some wild tales hereabouts." I asked her about the broken-bottle country, where Hides had had to collect rainwater with a canvas. She had carried a water bottle, she explained, and her feet had gotten tough from going barefoot.

The next day we managed a solid ten miles of river. In camp that evening the mood was buoyant again, mostly because Richard and Skip had forced Clive's hand and made the director agree to let us run the whole of the Tua. To persuade him, Richard had argued that the film itself would be a fraud if we were forced to pull out halfway: There was no way what we had done so far could be called a "great river journey."

On August 27 the BBC took the day off. Clive was unhappy with the interruption, but he could not abrogate his employees' union contract. For the first time we were free to run the river on our own schedule, to go as far as we could in a day. Clive would find us by helicopter on the 28th.

Our dash downriver turned into an incredible experience. By camp that evening, we had cov-

Whatever the effects of television orchestration, the white-water in New Guinea is real. Photo by Jim Slade/SOBEK.

ered 45 miles — as long a jaunt as any of the Sobek guides had ever made on any river in a single day. The rapids relented, and we found continuously swift current with only a few tricky spots. We passed out of the deep V-canyon we had started in and entered a zone of rolling jungle hills. The rock turned to basalt, then to a marbly conglomerate, and by nightfall we had glimpsed limestone that presaged the Purari. At midday we had traversed a curious and lovely stretch where the river was scored by longitudinal ribs of basalt. All day we watched lumbering black hornbills saw through the air, white cockatoos glide from limb to limb, and Brahminy kites loi-

ter in airborne helixes. A rare pair of cassowaries waddled across the stones on the right bank. The terrain seemed virtually uninhabited. Ten miles would go by before we would glimpse another ruined grass hut, half-claimed by jungle.

In the euphoria of camp, the guides began to talk mutiny. Screw the BBC, they said; instead of helicoptering out, we ought to go for it, take off downstream and live on our own resources. As caught up as I was in the happy solidarity of the group, the talk daunted me. The Purari threatened to be rougher than the roughest of the Tua, and there was no hope of escape before the flatland way station called Wabo, far downstream, beyond miles of desperate whitewater and unportageable canyon. In the last few days, despite my fear of water, I had consented to ride through several pugnacious rapids. In the middle of one, the prow of the boat had snagged on a rock. Suddenly the raft had pivoted backward, and we had been punched through a slot of fast water: The shore cliff screamed by inches from my head.

The next day life went back to normal. Clive was in by 9 A.M., but we didn't get on the river until almost one. We filmed a sequence in which, led by Richard, who hacked away at the foliage with a machete, we trudged through the underbrush carrying water cans, oars, and the like. Renée was relieved of one end of an oar on the orders of Clive, who didn't want her in that role.

In the meantime I had been reading more of Christina's book. On one page her horse waded belly-deep through mud; on another, she had her wrists tied to a makeshift raft by natives so that she could ford a dangerous river. Toward the end of her adventures a tribe on the Sepik initiated her in a brutal scarification ceremony in which a crocodile mark was carved into her shoulder. In the highlands an Englishman told her "that stories about Horse and Horse Lady had spread far and wide. He said that in our own way we were becoming part of the country's history, and that our travels would become a legend."

I found myself wondering whether Clive had read Christina's book. If he had, was he immune to natural skepticism? Was the fact that Christina was tall and blond the only thing that mattered for the movie? Richard told us that Clive's script followed Christina up the Sepik River (this journey to be filmed separately), across the headwaters divide, and down the Wahgi-Tua-Purari to the sea. The Sobek guides, apparently, were to

figure as mercenaries brought in to assist her with the tricky downstream bits. Christina would be featured traversing New Guinea from north to south. In the final scene she was supposed to wave goodbye as she stepped into a floatplane —just like in *Raiders of the Lost Ark*.

Mixed in with the talk of mutiny had been recurrent complaints about the "bullshit" we were being asked to collaborate in. And yet, I reflected glumly, ours was the very model of a modern expedition. The press conference at the North Pole, the 5.10 climber wired for sound, Neil Armstrong's self-conscious step for mankind—these are the emblems of the Decadent Age of Exploration. Sponsorship in itself need not condemn an expedition to compromise. After all, Columbus and Cortés had desperately sought patrons, and more than one conquistador had resorted to Bangsian Hype to scrape up cash and volunteers. But television and film had achieved new plateaus of manipulation and interference.

The paradox was that a good adventure documentary ought to capture exactly what it was like to run a wilderness river in New Guinea for the first time. But thanks to the arrogance of directors like Clive, the adventure itself was restructured to suit the film. The exploit of river running—all the craft and wit that went into every single stroke of the oar delivered by a Mike Boyle, a John Kramer, or a Skip Horner—was reduced to the pliable fiction of a "story element." We passengers in the boats, who were willing to risk our lives for a great adventure, became mere extras.

The helicopter made all the difference. It allowed an arbitrary definition of the start and end of our trip to supersede the natural one. It gave us an immense safety margin. It allowed us to cheat by leapfrogging past a tedious portage. It tempted us to bail out if the going got rough. And it served to insulate Clive from the humanity of the Sobek crew he was trying to maneuver from above, like plastic counters on a board game.

It seemed to me entirely fitting that Clive had announced his most important decision—to let us finish the Tua—from the front seat of his helicopter over the walkie-talkie to Richard. For if this is indeed the Decadent Age of Exploration, we have the airplane and the radio to blame for it. As late as 1953, when Everest was first climbed, there were basically no ground rules —any and all means that could be thrown into the attack were regarded as fair. And the exploring deed was still done in the innocence of isolation from the larger world. Nowadays it requires a deliberate atavism to keep exploring fresh. We agree to climb without pitons, to sail without a motor, to spelunk without dynamite. Flatter us with microphones, and we all sound like Neil Armstrong. Spoil us with helicopters, and we fantasize like Clive.

We pushed on down the Tua, while the BBC parked on a gravel bar miles ahead. Soon we had drifted into the limestone country, as canyon walls of mottled, contorted rock began to encroach. The river had grown to an immense size, and the current, Mike Boyle said, was the strongest he had ever rowed. The river was full of strange, squirrelly eddies.

Late in the afternoon we stopped to scout a rapid. Once we had accommodated to the scale, it looked terrifying, a pair of savage drops separated by only 30 yards. I chose at once to walk, as did Nick Nichols and Roger Brown, who had picture-taking as an excuse, as well as Richard Bangs, who simply didn't like the aura of the thing. I stood on a huge boulder on the flood-ravaged left bank to watch.

The first boat burst through in fine fashion, full of water but upright. Mike's came second. He missed the line on the upper drop by only a few feet and slid stern-first into a gigantic hidden hole. Mike was ripped from the oars and flung out of the boat, which danced for a few seconds, stood on its stern, then did a perfect "endo," or backward flip.

George Fuller surfaced yards from the boat, but Renée Goddard was trapped beneath it. She later said she thought that she was going to die. Instinct took over, however, and she walked herself by her hands out from under the raft even as it crashed through the second drop. Finally both she and George managed to crawl to shore. Mike had fortuitously popped up right beside the third boat, John Kramer's, and was instantly hauled aboard. They barely made it through the lower drop, then, without hesitation, set off in pursuit of the runaway raft.

Meanwhile Park, tired of playing taxi driver to the BBC, had been hovering to watch the action. When he saw the overturned raft heading downstream, he swooped to the left bank and motioned to Richard to jump in. Like cowboys in a corny western, they set off after the raft. John's boat seemed hardly to be gaining, and so, without much thought, Richard performed a stunt that may never before have been attempted—he leaped out of the moving helicopter onto the upside-down raft.

Richard slowed the runaway enough so that John and crew could catch up to it, but it took four men and half a mile to fight the thing into submission. Once they had it captured, Kramer lay in the bilge of his raft and gasped for breath.

Roger Brown had filmed the endo, but the best action of all escaped the camera. That night, our last on the Tua, we celebrated, but in a chastened mood. There was no further talk of turning our backs on the BBC and going for Wabo. A reconnaissance just below our camp revealed more of the same whitewater, and then much worse, including a canyon that Richard was sure would have been certain death. The next day we flew out, glad to have escaped disaster, proud of our effort despite the asterisks true candor would mark it with, and awed as never before by the river itself and by the deep wilderness into which we had so gingerly intruded.

A RIVER MYSTERY

By Scott Thybony

Fall, 1928, along *Grand Canyon's South Rim.* A Michigan tourist rushes up to a party of mounted sightseers on an isolated overlook. As he catches his breath, he tells the guide the group must go get help, fast. He's seen a boat with two people in it caught in a whirlpool on the Colorado River. It looked as though they were in trouble.

The dude wrangler listens impassively as the tourist tells him what he's seen: The people in the wooden scow had been forced to jump to the bank and haul their boat upriver. At the top of the eddy they'd leaped back in and tried to pole their way into the main current. Each time they tried, the eddy pulled them back. They looked trapped.

The guide isn't worried. Those people had hiked to the rim a couple of days before, he tells the tourist, and they know what they are doing. The sightseeing party continues on its way, unaware that that had been the last anyone saw of the couple struggling to break out of the eddy.

A month later army pilots flying 50 feet above the river spot a flat-bottomed scow. The boat had snagged away from shore several miles below Diamond Creek. It looks in good shape, but there is no sign of the missing couple.

1928, Green River, Utah. Glen and Bessie Hyde had put on the water on October 20. They billed their expedition as a honeymoon trip, though they were married six months before.

The Roaring Twenties were in full swing. Prohibition was fueling an underground economy, police had just seized four million dollars' worth of cocaine, and people were going into debt to maintain appearances. And it seemed that the days of real exploration had given way to dramatic stunts like going over waterfalls in barrels.

The year before, a party had run the Colorado —one of only a handful of successful expeditions since John Wesley Powell first ran it over a half-century before. As a publicity gimmick they took along a pet bear.

Glen and Bessie decided to pull a stunt that would land them a book contract and a sure ride

Bessie and Glen Hyde on the Colorado, 1928. Only they knew what happened on their voyage through the Grand Canyon, and —officially—neither lived to tell. Photo courtesy Emery Kolb collection, Special Collections Library, Northern Arizona University, Flagstaff.

on the lecture circuit. The Colorado was considered an extremely dangerous river in 1928. Their plan was to run it in a homemade boat, in record time, through the most notorious rapids in the world—without lifejackets. Bessie had never run a river before, but she was the first woman to attempt the Colorado. Glen was an Idaho rancher with limited experience. He had run the Salmon River and had floated the Fraser and Peace rivers in Canada. When reporters asked him why he wanted to go down the Colorado, he told them he wanted to give his bride a thrill.

The flat-bottomed scow was 20 feet long and 5 feet wide. Experienced boatmen said it looked like a coffin. It had long sweep oars rigged at the bow and stern. To travel fast its two passengers carried a mattress for sleeping onboard and a sand box they soaked with kerosene for cooking. They could save time by not setting up camp each evening.

Their trip went surprisingly well as far as Phantom Ranch. They hit a number of rocks but didn't damage the boat. Their only serious incident happened when Glen washed out in Sockdolager Rapid.

"We carried no life preservers," Bessie told a reporter. "I admit I was scared to death. I can't remember very clearly all that happened. All I know is that I managed somehow to hang onto the sweeps and keep the boat as straight as possible until my husband could grab the sides. Then I helped him aboard." They nicknamed their boat "Rain-in-the-Face" because it shipped so much water from the high waves.

The pair reached Phantom Ranch in record time. They had taken only 26 days to make it to the heart of the Grand Canyon. Bessie became the first woman to run Cataract Canyon and the upper portions of the Grand Canyon.

They hiked up the Bright Angel Trail to the South Rim to see Emery Kolb, a photographer who had twice run the Colorado. They were worried about what still lay ahead and wanted his advice. Kolb was surprised by the speed they had made. He was even more surprised when he learned they were not using lifejackets. He insisted they take his, but Glen refused. Kolb also offered to let the Hydes stay with him for the winter. It was mid-November and the cold weather was quickly approaching. Bessie was interested, but Glen wanted to push on.

Returning to the river, the Hydes met Adolph Sutro, a businessman from a well-known San Francisco family. They invited him to float with them the short distance to Hermit Creek where they had ordered supplies packed down to the river. Sutro was surprised at how carelessly they handled the boat and wondered how they had gotten as far as they had. Bessie seemed tired of the trip. At Hermit she'd nervously demanded they leave the river, but Glen forced her into the boat and pushed off.

Glen's father waited at Needles, California, for the couple to arrive as planned. When they were two weeks overdue, he contacted authorities. After the army pilots spotted the boat, Kolb, together with his brother and a park ranger, rebuilt an abandoned prospector's boat at the mouth of Diamond Creek and pushed into the river.

It was a cold, dangerous trip. At Mile 237 they found the Hydes' boat, intact, the bowline caught in the rocks away from shore. Although a foot of water lay in the bottom, everything else looked fine; there was no damage, no sign of violence. Food and clothing were stowed away along with a box camera, Glen's rifle, and Bessie's terse trip log. The last entry, dated November 30, mentioned bad rapids but gave no location. Since they had planned to write a book, it was odd that no detailed journal turned up. And although Bessie was an artist, the searchers did not find a sketchbook. Everything else was in place, yet the pair of adventurers had disappeared.

The search party continued downriver. Since they had only two lifejackets, Kolb's brother had strapped a five-gallon can on his back. At one point they came close to becoming victims themselves. Their boat flipped in Separation Rapids, throwing them all into the cold river. The ranger was pinned underneath momentarily and nearly drowned.

On Christmas day all hope of finding the couple alive was abandoned. Nothing indicating what had happened to the Hydes had surfaced. Kolb called off the river search. Meanwhile Mormon cowboys on the north rim of the canyon and Hualapai Indians on the south searched for footprints in the new snow without luck. Tracks, thought to be Glen's, were found at the foot of the Bass Trail by another river party.

Emery Kolb believed that Bessie must have been holding the bowline above Mile 232 rapid as Glen went ahead to scout. The current pulled her and the boat into the fast water, he speculated. When Glen saw her float past he dived in to save her, but they both drowned. Whatever happened to Bessie Hyde, she had been the first woman to run the Colorado River through the Grand Canyon, at least as far as Diamond Creek.

In a statement to the press, park superintendent Miner Tillostson warned "thrill seekers" to avoid future navigation of the river.

A year later the fathers of Glen and Bessie spent three weeks searching the north side of the canyon from Separation Rapid 31 miles upriver to the couple's last-known camp. It was a rough trip. They ran out of food but luckily found a prospector's cache and a trail that led them back to the rim. No clue to the missing Hydes turned up.

1971, below Lava Falls on the Colorado. It was a rough, low-water trip. Accidents had plagued the commercial river party. A young girl on the trip broke her arm in a run through Horn Creek Rapids. The next day she was evacuated by helicopter.

At their camp, a boatman began telling stories of earlier river disasters to distract the group from its own troubles. The oldest passenger, a woman called Liz who appeared to be in her late sixties, took a special interest in the story of the lost bride and groom, the guides said later. Liz, a short, feisty lady from somewhere in the East, had called the outfitter and asked to take the longest expedition available—a 20-day rowing trip. The company tried to talk her out of it, but she insisted. Even though it was rough, she enjoyed it and never complained. The boatmen remember her as being unusually knowledgeable about the river for a first-timer.

During the tale of Glen and Bessie's disappearance, Liz began adding details to the story that the boatmen had never heard. Someone asked her where she had heard all of this. She said she had known the couple before they attempted their trip. Then she began telling her version of what happened. In the middle of her story, wrapped in the mood of the river, she said she was Bessie Hyde. The river guides didn't believe her.

The trip was hard, she told them. Glen was a different person on the river. "He was a son of a bitch who beat me all the time," she told them. She wanted to back out of the trip when they reached Phantom Ranch, but Glen forced her to continue, she said. Things didn't improve in the lower canyon. She knew that her last chance to escape was at Diamond Creek, where a rough road reached the river.

When they pulled in above Diamond, she told Glen she was leaving. He refused to let her go. She then stabbed him with a kitchen knife, pushed him in the river, and let the boat drift away. She hiked out and caught a bus heading east and eventually changed her name.

The boatmen asked if she wasn't afraid of getting caught by telling her story. "I've lived my life," she said, "and nobody is going to believe me anyway."

O.C. Dale was one of the boatmen who listened to her story that night. He still believes she was only joking. But another river guide on the trip,

The 20-foot scow Bessie and Glen Hyde rode down the Colorado. Only the scow and a mystery survived the trip. Photo courtesy Emery Kolb collection, Special Collections Library, Northern Arizona University, Flagstaff.

George Billingsley, is convinced there is a good chance Liz was actually Bessie Hyde. At the time she told her story, George wasn't very familiar with the history of the Hydes' disappearance. Yet much of what he has learned about the case since fits the story Liz told that night by the campfire.

The circumstantial evidence is intriguing. Liz is Bessie's age and height; she lives near Bessie's hometown. On her "first" Colorado River trip, she was able to relate a convincing story about Bessie Hyde on the spur of the moment.

Years after her river trip, I called Liz at her home. She was able to recount details of the 1971 trip that the boatmen had forgotten, but when asked about the Hydes' disappearance she denied having told the story. "I don't remember that at all," she said matter-of-factly. "I'm not Bessie. I don't even know the name Hyde."

The real story will probably never be known. Mike Harrison, a former park ranger who had met Glen and Bessie when they hiked out of the canyon, was asked if he thought Bessie could still be alive. He didn't think so. "In those days," he said, "the river never gave up its dead. Never."

RUNNING WILBERFORCE CANYON

By Bill Mason

My idea of the perfect river is one that has a spectacular falls or canyon, or both, preferably near the end, so you've got something to look forward to, like icing on the cake. And if there's a canyon a couple of miles long and over 200 feet deep below the falls, with rapids that might be runnable, well, that would be the river of which dreams are made.

The Hood is such a river. It flows due east through Canada's Northwest Territories for about 100 miles before swinging north and emptying into the Arctic Ocean at Bathurst Inlet. About a day's journey above the mouth, the river narrows into a red sandstone canyon, then plunges 80 feet into a churning cauldron of foam, takes a right-angle turn to the left and plunges again, over a 100-foot drop. The two drops are Wilberforce Falls, perhaps the most spectacular in Canada. Towering spires soar from the very base of the second falls, high above the first. If you climb out along the narrow hogback ridge that provides access to one of the pinnacles, you can look down 180 feet into the depths of the canyon.

In 1985, six of us ran the Hood. Wally Schaber and I were in one canoe, Alan Whatmough and Bruce Cockburn in the second, and Gilles Couet and Gilles Levesque in the third. Because of its remoteness and its frigid water and air temperatures, the Hood is in a class by itself as a wilderness experience. It was the middle of July, and we still had to dodge ice on all the big lakes. You can imagine what that did for the water temperatures downstream. We ran the more difficult rapids with considerable apprehension.

But the whitewater we were waiting for was the canyon below Wilberforce Falls. If it were runnable, it would be beyond our wildest dreams. Below the two falls, the Hood surges through a two-mile canyon below 200-foot walls on its journey to the ocean.

The canoeists prepare to put in below Wilberforce Falls on Canada's Hood River, lured by the unrun canyon below. Photo by Bill Mason.

We pitched camp above the falls in the pouring rain, then rushed off to have a look at the canyon. We found the scree slope that led to the base of the falls, then walked along the canyon rim, scouting rapids. They looked difficult, but we believed we could handle them, and we worked out an intricate plan of back-ferries and lines of attack. Once we got into the canyon there would be no lining or portaging and no turning back. The walls were either sheer, or steep, crumbling rock with overhangs.

As I retraced my steps along the canyon rim, I estimated the degree of difficulty and multiplied by two. Rapids always look much easier from above; waves flatten out and don't look as forbidding as they really are. I knew running those rapids deep within the canyon was going to be exciting. Schaber, Couet, and Levesque were ecstatic about the idea. Alan volunteered to photograph the run from above.

We waited out a rainy night and the next day left the canoes at the top of the scree slope, carried all the gear over the three-mile portage in the rain and set up camp at the end of the canyon.

Even though we would be wearing wetsuits and paddling jackets, no one was very keen on attempting the canyon in cold, rainy weather. With water temperatures just above freezing, the dangers of hypothermia would have been too great. But there was also a psychological factor. The black depths of that canyon just looked too intimidating in this bleak weather.

In the morning, the sky was clear. We rushed through breakfast, put on our wetsuits, and set out for the head of the canyon, scouting the rapids again as we went. We looked for eddies. They would give us a chance to catch our breath and to bail, but there were very few. The river looked powerful, but each rapid on its own looked runnable. The holes were avoidable, the V's clearly defined. The haystacks would give us a good ride.

We eased the boats down the scree slope. Schaber and I reached water level just as Couet and Levesque completed their front ferry to the right side of the canyon below the falls. Their skill was impressive: the water rushing downstream from the base of the falls was a seething mass of boils. The back eddy by shore raced upstream at an alarming angle. I didn't like it, and the anxiety in Wally's voice reinforced my apprehension. We would have to set an extreme angle when we exited the eddy or be drawn back toward the falls.

With the canoe facing upstream, we climbed in and began our front-ferry, but were pulled quickly toward the falls. We back-paddled furiously but went nowhere. Finally, Wally grabbed onto some rocks and dragged the canoe and me back to the eddy. On the fourth try we made it out. The boils pulled and grabbed the canoe as we ferried across the current. We were definitely not having a good time. The sheer volume and turbulence were very unsettling. We had completely underestimated the power of the water. But now that we had ferried to the far shore, there was no turning back.

We gazed up at Alan, a slim speck against the sky on the canyon rim. Levesque and Couet pushed off, ran down the side of the first rapid

Wilberforce Falls plunges into the top of the canyon on the Hood River in Canada's Northwest Territories. Photo by Bill Mason.

**Gilles Couet and Gilles Levesque start their run of Wilberforce Canyon. Their canoe
would make it through, empty but unscathed; they would climb out. Photo by Bill Mason.**

and eddied out just around the bend. As we crossed the eddy line, we felt our stern sinking into a whirlpool. It was not a good feeling. This stuff was big! Bigger than anything we had ever paddled, and this was the first rapid, the one that had appeared the easiest. We should have multiplied the degree of difficulty by four or five.

By the time we pulled into the eddy with Couet and Levesque, we had lost our enthusiasm for our carefully made plans. All we wanted to do was get on with it. We paddled out of the eddy, shot by the other boat, and began to back-ferry to set up for the next rapid. It would have been a wild, exhilarating ride anywhere else, but here

worry outweighed pleasure. I managed a half-hearted shout and reached under my spray skirt to get my camera out. "Forget the pictures!" Wally shouted. I looked back to protest just as the third rapid came into view. In the history of picture-taking, no camera ever went back into its box faster.

In front of us, the whole river was piling into a cliff. Schaber yelled for a back-ferry to the right. We hugged the right side of the V, which put us into the diagonal waves coming off the standing waves. We hit the diagonals broadside. The canoe rolled up on its side and without even a pause just kept going over. One instant I was upright and the next I was hanging upside down. I kicked against the bottom of the canoe, propelling myself down and out of the spray skirt.

I struggled for the surface but there was no air, only turbulence and whitewater. My first breath was half air and half water. I was pulled under, and when I finally got another breath I caught sight of Schaber. The canoe was between us and he was swinging toward the right shore. We rode the waves of one rapid after another until I saw the blue water racing for a drop-off and a hole. I kicked away from it and lost sight of Wally as the waves engulfed me. Then I was through the worst of the rapid. Schaber was nowhere to be seen.

Suddenly, I felt the cold and the fatigue. I swung close to the right bank and pulled myself onto a ledge about a foot above water. I wondered about Schaber, Couet, and Levesque, but could see no one. I saw no alternative, so I started to climb out of the canyon. I went as far as I could, but was stopped cold under a crumbly overhang and had to climb down. Back by the river, warm finally from exertion, I heard Schaber call from the rim above me. He had washed through a hole that had sucked his running shoes off his feet and had climbed out of the canyon in his wetsuit boots. At his direction, I swam to the other side of the river and was able to make an easier climb up the other cliff.

We headed for our camp, Wally on one side of the rim, I on the other. When our tents came into sight, I saw four figures. Everyone was accounted for, and we soon heard the full story. Couet and Levesque had seen us capsize and rushed to shore to search for us. As they peered downstream, their canoe drifted into view on the current. They had pulled it up to a ledge but a wave had lifted it free. With considerable consternation they watched it negotiate the rapid that had trashed Wally and me and then dance merrily on its way around a bend. Then they swam to the other side of the river and climbed out of the canyon. Schaber eventually spotted their canoe in an eddy below the rapids and paddled it to shore by the camp. And Couet later found the boat we had lost and was able to pry it off a rock a couple of miles downstream. The spray cover was torn, paddles gone and Schaber's camera was missing.

There was much discussion that night about our canoeing skills. There we were with our complete spray skirt, back-ferry, high and low braces, pries and draws, pivots and backwatering, and we ended up swimming. A canoe with no spray cover and no paddlers ran everything and came through dry. It was agreed that we would have been better off just to skip the paddling and lie down in our boat.

Now when I remember the canyon below Wilberforce Falls, I am sure we have run bigger stuff with flotation in the canoe and even played in it. So why was it such a harrowing experience? Why did I try to climb out of the canyon where I was instead of swimming across immediately to the easier climb?

What made it such a nightmare was the combination of all the elements. We were many hundreds of miles from help. We could not have replaced a lost canoe. The water was icy. To enter a canyon is to go where there is no return. Having made shore, I was helpless. There was an irresistible urge to escape the canyon; we all felt it.

And then there is the old question: Why venture into a canyon like that? Why take the risk? Is it worth it? Well, there's the incredible view from the bottom of the canyon looking up as we round each bend in the river. There's the sheer thrill of running whitewater. We had wondered if we would be the first to run this stretch. The arctic shore just north of where we were is dotted with the graves of the almost 200 men who died in the attempt to be the first through the Northwest Passage. But for us being first was no big deal. We'd just wanted to run it. We didn't need a reason.

In the end, it was worth it because everything came out all right. If we had lost a canoe or if one of us had been hurt or killed, it would not have been worth it. Sooner or later someone will run it. Maybe even in a canoe, probably at lower water.

One thing Wally and I feel bad about is that we'll never know whether Couet and Levesque could have made the run. We think they could have. In any case, if you meet them on the streets of Chicoutimi (Quebec) and ask how they made out in Wilberforce Canyon, they can honestly say: "Oh, the canoe went through just fine. Hardly a drop of water in it."

KAYAKING IN THE CALIFORNIA FAST LANE

By Chuck Stanley

The glory of river first descents leans heavily on their association with mountaineering first ascents. Who can deny the accomplishment of being the first to attain the summit of the Matterhorn after so many had tried and failed? But first descents, unfortunately, almost always go to the first boaters who manage to find the put-in. To the chagrin of true whitewater experts, it's easy to fall downstream; even a log can make it. Despite all this, most kayakers involved in first descents have the delusion that they alone possess the special skills, vision, and perseverance required to accomplish the impossible.

In March of 1980, Bald Rock Canyon on the Middle Fork of the Feather River and the Golden Gate section of the South Fork of the American River, both on the west slope of the Sierra Nevada, were the Matterhorn and Eiger of California river running. Naturally, Lars Holbek, Richard Montgomery, and I felt we alone possessed the skill and guts to do them. But the first descent scene was undergoing major upheaval. We had always had our pick of fine first runs; now we were being challenged by upstarts, a couple of groups of determined advanced paddlers and a crew of retired rock climbers. The advanced guys were too scared to really conquer the drops in the big canyons, and although the old rock climbers weren't afraid of

In 1980, Bald Rock Canyon on the Middle Fork of the Feather River was the Matterhorn of Sierra kayaking. With good reason: Lars Holbek protrudes from the foam of a hole in one of the canyon's Class V sections. Photo by John Armstrong.

the canyons, they didn't like to get wet; they specialized in portaging across the Sierras.

The name Golden Gate came from Charlie Martin's assessment of it in his guidebook, *Sierra Whitewater*, as "a novel substitute for jumping off the Golden Gate Bridge." In Bald Rock Canyon, Martin had written, boaters would find "insurmountable problems." We planned to run both on our spring vacation from college.

A week before we were set to go, we heard that the Magneson brothers, John and Eric, were planning to run Golden Gate. After cramming all day for a midterm, I set down my tenth cup of coffee and jittered over to the pay phone. As Lars listened in, I interrogated John Magneson about his plans. My coffee-addled brain raced through the options. Should we ask them to join our trip, or tell them it was just too hard for them? I fumbled for an answer. Finally I blurted out that I would deck anyone I found at the put-in, slammed down the receiver, and went for another cup of coffee. Lars was mortified! I had committed a major breach of first-descent etiquette. It's one thing to lie about your plans, but you simply can't threaten rival paddlers. Lars convinced me to call back Magneson. I did, and after a rambling five-minute apology, again promised to deck anyone at the put-in and slammed down the receiver.

Immediately, we changed our plans and headed straight for the Golden Gate on Friday afternoon in Holbek's '56 VW van, floored—45 m.p.h.! It was going to be a week of first descents.

We set up our ten-speed-bike shuttle and arrived at the put-in. With relief I noted no sign of the Magnesons. Eric could easily deck *me* with one hand. We were also relieved to see that the river was low, about 400 cfs, a level that would allow us to make midstream stops and portages in the steep-walled gorges.

The three of us approached first-descent river running as a team. We were ready for this kind of water because we were world-class kayakers! My claim to fame was that I was an also-ran slalom racer who had twice managed to sneak onto the U.S. team for the world championships and had won the 1980 K-1 nationals. Lars never raced much, but he could paddle as well as I, and Richard wasn't far behind. And we were all in our early twenties and in killer shape.

Our technique was to move quickly, scouting from our boats. We would communicate only by eye contact as we eddy-hopped down the rapids. No yelling. No flailing hand signals except for the vector. After running a drop, the leader would face upstream and extend his arm to point out the proper line to those above. Expert boat-handling skills made our team work.

Once on the water we found the Golden Gate to be a typical Sierran granite Class V with big-boulder drops followed by beautiful calm pools. As usual, we had the problem of too many leaders! We would race down the flatwater sections to the lip of the next big drop, where we would mill around desperately looking for routes so no one else could have the honor of going first. About three miles down, just below the rapid called Drainpipe, Richard hit a subsurface rock at the bottom of a seven-foot drop with such force that he severely sprained his ankle. Only three miles into a nine-mile journey, he was unable to portage his boat. Either Lars or I had to carry it. Because he couldn't walk well, Richard was even reluctant to scout unless it was absolutely necessary. This led to a spectacular wipeout at the rapid we dubbed Straight Shot. Richard didn't scout the drop, relying on Lars's report of an easy run down the middle. Unfortunately, he hit the ten-foot-wide slot sideways. His boat jammed

Scouting Bald Rock means climbing house-sized granite boulders for a better view. At river level, granite slabs and boulders; above, more granite slabs and cliffs. Photo by John Armstrong.

briefly and then it and Richard disappeared, to surface seconds later, the kayak bent in half like a taco.

We straightened out the boat and things went better. Richard decided that it was worth a bit of pain to scout the rapids and we quickly portaged those that looked unreasonable. Fortunately, the Golden Gate failed to live up to its name. By nine that night we were safely at a hospital emergency room waiting for Richard's foot to be X-rayed. After several hours of waiting with various moaning victims of car accidents and bar fights, Richard's ankle was declared unbroken. We then

declared him fit for more first descenting. We were off to Bald Rock Canyon!

We arrived at Brush Creek late in the afternoon of the next day after another long drive in the VW bus. Here we stashed the ten-speed in the bushes and ventured down the 7-mile dirt road to Milsap Bar, the put-in. The bike would be our shuttle, after a 20-mile hitchhike on the main highway.

We had one of Lars's VW-home-cooked meals of brown rice and lentils, washed down with our favorite beer, Brown Derby, the cheapest available in the Free World. After dinner, we organized our gear. In Bald Rock Canyon, granite walls form the shoreline, so Lars prepared his rock-climbing equipment. Much to our dismay, he had forgotten to bring the hardware; all we had were a few old slings and our crummy polypropylene throw ropes. Lars and Richard decided to save weight by bringing no overnight gear, and no extra clothes or food. I was a bit more pessimistic about our chances of paddling 6.5 miles of Class V water and 13 miles of lake, hitchhiking 20 miles, and then riding the bike 7 miles down the dirt road to Milsap Bar, all in one day. I brought a sleeping bag and ground cloth. Our first-aid kit consisted of duct tape and our emergency gear of one old plastic rafting paddle. All this was tossed into our Hollowforms, which had never felt the dead weight of float bags. What we lacked in equipment we hoped to make up for with skill.

Around the campfire we celebrated our successful run. While Lars and I drank Brown Derby and bragged about our glorious first descent of the suicidal Golden Gate, Richard, a slightly introspective math nut with the physique of Michelangelo's *David*, sat in the van pondering his math book. Richard enjoys the mental athletics of high mathematics as much as he loves the world of whitewater, but Lars dwells in the physical world. He's big, strong, bold, and funny. He is an expert rock climber and kayaker, and he naturally assumes the role of leader when the rapids get tough and the canyon walls climb. He also assumes the role of leader the rest of the time; it can drive you nuts. I'm a bit of an enigma: bold yet shy, confident but scared, and skinny but tough. When the going gets tough, I like Lars to lead.

The next morning dawned overcast and cool. It was not ideal weather to run the most rugged canyon any of us had ever attempted. To complicate matters, the river was flowing at 1,500 cfs, much too high for a first descent. The mood was somber during our breakfast of oatmeal. As I loaded my sleeping bag into my kayak I had the feeling that I would be needing it.

After breakfast and the associated milling around, we managed to get on the water by 9 A.M. I'll never forget the sense of foreboding I felt as I slipped into my kayak. Above swirled ominous gray clouds, in front of me was a pulsating river, and downstream in the distance were the towering granite walls of Bald Rock Canyon. The water was powerful, and an ample side creek added to the flow. Ahead lay the unknown river flowing through a granite gorge with 2,000-foot walls. The only information we had about the run had been gleaned from topographical maps. The river's mile-by-mile gradient was 55, 60, 90, 140, 195, 95, and 80 feet per mile, and the canyon walls were vertical for the two steepest miles.

The first mile was easy Class III and provided no opportunity to paddle out my sense of foreboding. The first challenge was an easy Class V rapid; here the river made an even, long drop, with rocks and big waves. Near the end of the drop there was what looked to be a soft, punchable hole. Richard scouted it, lined up at the top, and entered the rapid with precision. Once on the approach to the hole, he floored it, hit the hole full speed and was stopped dead. After a couple of quick bounces he pulled free and finished the drop. It was now very clear we were running a real river.

When we regrouped, the mood was tense. All three of us love big water and riding holes. But nobody enjoys getting backendered at the lip of an unknown rapid, or blowing a spray cover and missing the last eddy above a falls. We all knew that big water, extreme river gradient, and vertical granite walls were a recipe for disaster.

We ran the next mile of Class IV river without mishap, but the farther we paddled, the taller the canyon walls loomed. I took account of our situation: the water was too high, the weather was overcast and cool. We were only two miles into the run so we could still hike back upstream to the put-in. Continuing beyond this point meant that we were committed to the run. We were at the point of no return.

Before I got out of my boat to scout the next drop, I decided that I wanted out of there. Better to return on a nice hot spring day. When I reached the scouting spot, most of the good parking spaces were taken. I precariously balanced my boat on a slab of sloping granite. I hadn't walked more than 20 feet before I heard the sickening sound of plastic on rock. I turned to see my boat heading downstream! I decided not to jump in and risk swimming an unscouted rapid to save the kayak. This made my decision to bail out easy—I was off the hook! To my dismay, Lars jumped in heroically at the last second and swam my boat to shore just before the drop. I was back on the hook.

Lars bounded downstream to scout the next rapid; Richard and I talked over our situation. With little discussion, we decided it would be best to bail out and hike back upstream. We announced our decision to quit. Lars simply informed us that he would continue solo, and wished us luck. Richard and I were stunned. Faced with running Lars's shuttle, we decided to continue.

After a quick scout, we selected our route down Point of No Return Rapid. Following Lars's lead,

I shot down the right side, threading the needle between a boiling cushion and a nasty ledge hole. The tension broke when Lars and I looked upstream to see Richard pogo vertically on the boil while windmilling his paddle frantically. It was a sight out of a Road Runner cartoon. When Richard landed upright and joined us in the eddy below, we all had a good laugh. Knowing that our only option was to keep moving downstream, we relaxed a bit.

The next mile of rapids and scenery was fantastic. On both sides of the river giant granite slabs and boulders formed the streambed. The rapids varied from beautiful Class V boulder gardens to a series of river-wide slides that emptied into giant punch bowl pools. Below the slides, a fun Class III boulder garden led into a gorge.

As we rounded the curve, I knew we were in trouble. Downstream, vertical walls towered above. In the river lay several house-sized boulders, and below them the bottom dropped out—a waterfall. We paddled as far as we dared and took out on river right. From there we walked 50 yards downstream until the walls stopped us at the lip of a 10-foot vertical drop. Just below the drop was a short pool and then a 30-foot waterfall. Above the drop, the far shore offered no portage route, but there was a small eddy at the lip of the falls that would give us access to a potential carry on river left. From our vantage point we couldn't see if it would go. The short pool between the 10-foot drop and the waterfall was interrupted by three jets of fast water that shot between boulders and then over the falls. Our options were to rock climb out of the canyon or to cross to river left and attempt to portage.

We decided to send someone paddling across at the lip of the falls to reconnoiter, but first we

had to lower the paddler and his boat to a small, sloping ledge that could be used as a launching pad.

The first chore was to set a rappel anchor above the drop. Although Lars had forgotten the climbing hardware, he still had his ingenuity. We spent the next half hour watching him attempt to set a British-style nut using a stone tied into a piece of webbing. After many failures, he finally declared the anchor set.

Lars and Richard decided that I, the hotshot power-paddling slalom racer, should volunteer to paddle across to the scouting spot. Being a coward at heart, I wasn't thrilled at the prospect, but somebody had to go.

As I lowered myself hand-over-hand down the rope, water cascaded over the falls and onto my head. Once I reached the precarious ledge at the bottom, Lars lowered my boat to me, and I got in without mishap. Before me lay the most frightening ferry of my life. The task was to cross the entire river just 20 feet above the falls. To go over was sure death. From my kayak I looked across the river at my goal, a small eddy whose entrance was guarded by a fence of small rocks. Between me and the eddy ran the three fast chutes separated by boiling eddies behind the boulders. I took a deep breath, blasted across the first jet, and landed with a snap in the first midstream eddy. Below me lay the waterfall. Ahead were two more jets, and two more eddies I had to catch. I was scared, but the fact that the second jet was no worse than the first bolstered my confidence. I blasted across into the relative safety of the second midstream eddy and surveyed my predicament. Only one more move to go. Although the

last jet was the slowest of the three, some small rocks protected the entrance to the final eddy. I would have to power straight into it. Any miscalculation of angle or speed would have dire consequences. If I hit one of the fence rocks, I would spin out and be swept over the falls. My deepest fear wasn't that I would botch the move, but that I would discover it was impossible to portage on river left; then I'd have to repeat the harrowing ferry to join Lars and Richard for the climb out of the canyon. After considering the options, I put my faith in my skill and equipment. I floored it across the jet and shot between the rocks to safety! I looked back; Lars and Richard were smiling.

I got out of my kayak quickly and scampered downstream on a beautiful granite slab around giant boulders. Fifty yards below, I rounded the last boulder and saw a flat pool and a reasonable put-in. Below was a half mile of runnable rapids. We had passed the crux!

I ran gleefully back to Lars and Richard and let them know with a "yahoo!" that it was a go. Their smiles faded as they viewed the ferry before them. Richard lowered himself down to the ledge and Lars sent down his kayak. Richard climbed in and waited. Lars decided to rappel off the boulder while in his boat. At first he was able to control his downward speed, but as the boulder became steeper, he slid faster until he was freefalling. The flying kayak landed smack on Richard's head! Fortunately, no one was hurt. After collecting the rope, the two made their way safely across the river. Reunited, we gaped at the waterfall—an explosion of water on rock that we dubbed Atom Bomb Falls.

Below the falls, we made good time, paddling

Lars Holbek "ski jumps" a drop. Photo by John Armstrong.

Lars Holbek below Curtain Falls, one of the last drops before the
river flows into Oroville Reservoir. Photo by John Armstrong.

many of the rapids and portaging quickly any that required too much time to scout properly. But we had spent three hours getting around Atom Bomb Falls and it was getting late. Although harried, we marveled at the grandeur around us. To the right was Bald Rock Dome, a granite monolith like those in Yosemite Valley. To our left, granite slabs towered skyward. About a mile below Atom Bomb Falls, the river curved left at the base of Bald Rock Dome. Around this curve I saw a horizon line and the frothing mist that could be made only by a big waterfall.

Carefully, we caught the eddy at the lip of the falls and climbed out of our boats. At our feet was Curtain Falls, a 30-foot plunge over a river-wide granite slab into a big granite punch bowl. Immediately below is the Super Slide, where the river hurtles down a 10-foot-high, low-angle ramp into a king-sized hole. The runout is another giant granite punch bowl. Unbelievable! We portaged hastily. In our race against darkness we found it quicker to carry around most of the rapids for the next mile.

Richard's sprained ankle was beginning to wear out. To hasten his progress, I portaged both of our kayaks while he hobbled over the boulders. About a mile above the Lake Oroville Reservoir the rapids eased to Class IV, but we were getting so tired we were up to running only the most straightforward ones. About halfway through a portage Lars exclaimed, "It's only a goddamn Class IV!" and carried back upstream to run it. Richard and I figured it was faster to carry.

We reached the lake at dusk only to find a half-mile-long logjam. After half an hour of toil through logs and debris we hit the open water and began the 13-mile lake paddle. We took turns riding each other's wakes, and made good time. We arrived at our take-out at midnight. The hitchhiking looked bleak.

With the satisfaction that comes with an unspoken I-told-you-so, I unpacked my tarp and down sleeping bag. Lars and Richard gathered firewood as I set up the tarp and fluffed the bag. Since I'm a good sport, I suggested that they could snuggle with me under the tarp. After half an hour of shivering, they huddled around the fire for the rest of the night, doing jumping jacks, uprooting

a highway sign for firewood and generally making it tough for me to sleep. Dawn broke none too soon.

After catching a ride, Lars completed the shuttle quickly and we were on our way to another first descent.

We drove to the Bear River, near Auburn, where the VW broke down and Richard and I spent two days drinking coffee and studying while Lars pulled the engine in the Safeway parking lot and fixed the problem.

Then we did our first and last descent of the Bear River, from Highway 49 to Camp Far West Reservoir. Lars got lost riding the shuttle on his bike, we didn't put in until 1 P.M., and had to bivouac around a campfire that night.

Three first descents, two of them classics. We called it our 49'er week, not because it was done in gold country, but for the 49 portages it took us to get down those rivers!

Since then, we've returned and run Bald Rock Canyon and Golden Gate with better style. As of this writing only Atom Bomb Falls remains unrun.

RIVER EXPLORATION IN THE SOUTHERN APPALACHIANS

By Payson Kennedy

In the summer of 1952, Hugh Caldwell was working at Camp Merrie-Woode in the mountains of southwestern North Carolina. Merrie-Woode was one of the oldest girls' camps in the South, and one of its specialties was canoeing. Most of the trips were on tame water, and Caldwell set out to find some more challenging rivers.

He consulted a highway map and found a river running between South Carolina and nearby Georgia, only a few miles from Merrie-Woode, called the Chattooga. Caldwell had never heard of it, but there were bridges at Georgia 28 and US 76, and the section between them looked to Caldwell like a good length for a day trip.

Unlike most mountain rivers, the Chattooga is very easy at the start, but gets more difficult as you descend it. Caldwell didn't know that, however, as he started out in his keeled 18-foot Grumman aluminum canoe, not the best craft for a mountain stream. He didn't know much else about the Chattooga, either, certainly not that in 20 or so years it would be one of the best-known whitewater rivers in the South. He had consulted no topo maps; he was alone; he had no lifejacket. In short, he says, "I violated almost every river standard now in practice."

Caldwell had a long day. Intermittent heavy rain made things more uncomfortable and raised the river level. By midafternoon, he had stopped scouting rapids because he was afraid he wouldn't reach the take-out before dark. He broached once on what was to become known to latter-day boaters as Painted Rock. The Grumman bent, but it didn't fold. It was stuck though, and Caldwell lost much time in freeing it. Then he blundered into the now-famous Bull Sluice. It was near dark. He couldn't stop to scout so he took what appeared to be the best line. The rapid's hydraulic caught him, filled the boat and flushed boat and paddler out the bottom chute. Caldwell was only a quarter mile from the take-out he was aiming for, but he didn't know it. "So I was pretty discouraged," he says.

It was dark when he finally pulled his canoe up onto the beach at US 76. From the time he started at dawn, he had not seen another human being on the river that today, on a good weekend, is filled with paddlers.

But that was the way whitewater boating was in the Southeast during the pioneering decades of this century, when rivers were being run for the first time: simple equipment, lots of nerve and energy, and not too much experience. It was a combination that took boaters through first descents all over the region.

Our historical research revealed, as expected, that dugout canoes built by the Cherokees who inhabited the region were used only for ferrying across the rivers: no accounts exist of their use for transportation up and down the rivers—even on the flatter stretches. Surviving Cherokee canoes and drawings of the dugouts suggest they were probably sluggish to paddle, heavy to portage, and unsuitable for whitewater. Likewise, there is little evidence to suggest that the northern Indians or the French trappers traveled to the southeast in their more maneuverable and riverworthy birchbark canoes. And we found no record of early explorers or settlers using canoes in their travels into the mountains.

Although whitewater paddling in the Southern Appalachians appears to have begun sometime before 1914, until the fifties communication between paddlers was limited to small groups of friends. Hence, it is difficult to determine with any confidence who actually made the first runs on various rivers. Many paddlers made exploratory runs without knowledge of earlier trips. Thus lots of us have had the thrills, challenge, and satisfaction of thinking we might be making first descents.

In researching those days, my richest sources of information were the old-time paddlers themselves, many of whom were associated with the outstanding canoeing programs at summer camps in the mountains of North Carolina and Georgia.

One of the undisputed pioneers was Frank Bell, who began canoeing in 1914 as a camper at French Broad Camp in North Carolina. Still active today at 90, Bell has sharp recollections of those early times. In 1914, he made his first river trip down the French Broad from Brevard to Asheville. In 1922 Bell founded Camp Mondamin, in western North Carolina, where whitewater paddling played a prominent role from the beginning. The following year, he organized a trip with a counselor named George Blackburn and three campers that was probably the first descent of the full length of the French Broad—nearly a thousand miles. The group went down the river from Mud Creek near Hendersonville, North Carolina, to the Tennessee and Ohio rivers, and on to the Mississippi at Cairo, Illinois. There was then only one dam on this entire route and the trip took about a month.

Bell canoed with the group through all of the whitewater sections and then returned to his camp duties. In rough water, the loaded cedar and canvas canoes swamped and overturned many times, forcing the paddlers to stop frequently for repairs. Since there was no extra flotation in the canoes and none of the paddlers wore lifejackets, getting themselves and the loaded boats to shore was none too easy. Often, they lost supplies and gear, and replacing them turned into a sort of scavenger hunt as they continued on their way. Since they had no specialized canoeing or camping equipment, they could usually replace things without much difficulty. They carried blankets rather than sleeping bags, a few items of clothing, and a minimal supply of food and cooking equipment. Once Bell used a

Frank Bell on the Toxaway-Keowee River in South Carolina. In those days, equipment was simple or, in the case of life jackets, missing entirely. But the love of whitewater was as great as at any time. Photo courtesy Frank Bell, Sr.

wagon wheel iron from a blacksmith shop, bent to the shape of the bow, to hold the front of a canoe together. He and his companions then carved thwarts from tree limbs and used ropes between the gunwales to hold the sides in. Finally, they patched the leaks with tar.

The most memorable event of the trip for Bell was the attempt to run a difficult rapid near Hot Springs, North Carolina. After scouting it, three of the five paddlers portaged, but Bell and a camper ran it tandem. The canoe filled in the standing waves on the approach and was sucked underwater in a powerful whirlpool. The current pushed the camper toward shore, but Bell, near

exhaustion, was carried downstream. He had nearly given up, when his foot touched the bottom and he struggled onto the rocks. Stories of this event made the rounds, and a Class IV rapid about a mile above Hot Springs was named Frank Bell's Rapid. Oddly enough, Bell is sure that this is not the one he and the camper had overturned in. Since there are no similar rapids in the vicinity, he believes that theirs could lie under one of the small dams upstream of Hot Springs.

Fifty years later, in 1973, Bell led another Camp Mondamin group on a trip through the best whitewater section of the French Broad.

On another early trip, Bell and Bill Childs

made what was probably a first descent of the Green River in North Carolina. They put in below Lake Summit Powerhouse and soon entered a narrow, steep-walled gorge in which the river plunged precipitously over ledges and boulders, at one point dropping more than 300 feet in a mile. Within the first 2 miles, their canoe was completely destroyed and the two continued on foot, walking, scrambling, and swimming the remainder of the 16 miles to Lake Adger.

Perseverance was an important attribute in those days. When Bell paddled the Tuckasegee River in southwestern North Carolina in the 1930s, before Fontana Dam was built, he and his partner, Billy Pratt, overturned in a long, powerful rapid and washed through it before they could reach shore. They walked back upstream but were unable to find any sign of their canoe. Finally, they noticed a huge boulder that split the main current, swam to it and began feeling around it with their feet as they held onto the rock and each other. They were able to just touch the pinned canoe, wrapped around the rock underwater. After much tugging and prying, they were able to recover only a few splintered fragments.

As Bell knew, river exploration at the time was a fairly risky and expensive endeavor, tough on canoes and paddlers alike. The canoes were not only much more fragile than today's, but they were comparatively much much more expensive. A cedar and canvas Old Town cost about $150 then. But Bell said he could employ as many laborers as he needed at the camp for ten cents an hour, so a canoe represented 1,500 hours of labor. At least the accessories were cheap: no special flotation or outfitting, no lifejackets, helmets or special clothing were used. The only equipment, other than the boat, was a paddle, usually a surprisingly long one. Bell keeps a 6-foot-two-inch spruce paddle in his living room as a memento of the 1923 French Broad trip.

When they finally arrived on the scene, aluminum canoes made exploration easier, but they sometimes fared no better than canvas ones. Hugh Caldwell remembers an early run on the Chattooga in which he ran the rapid called Jawbone with Fritz Orr, Jr., Al Barrett, and Bunny Johns (then Bunny Bergin, a canoeing counselor at Merrie-Woode). He waited below to photograph Orr making the run. Orr's canoe came through upside down and went over the next drop, Sock-Em-Dog. He was all right, but when Caldwell scrambled over the boulders to catch the boat in the washout, there was no canoe. "It had simply disappeared," said Caldwell. Half an hour later a canteen that had been tied to the canoe appeared downstream. "With darkness approaching," said Caldwell, "we gave up on the lost canoe. One more rapid and we were in Lake Tugaloo. The next day we came back with ropes and grappling irons but found no trace of our lost canoe."

River exploration was hard on the paddlers, too. In 1933, Bell led a Mondamin trip that began below the Green River Gorge and continued down the Green to the Broad, the Congaree, the Santee, and on to the Atlantic. After leaving the Green's whitewater, they encountered a problem that few whitewater paddlers have to worry about today: several of them developed malaria. Caldwell remembers that for days after his first trip on the Chattooga his elbow joints were so sore from drawing the cumbersome Grumman that it hurt to raise a glass of water.

From 1934 to 1937 Caldwell spent his summers at Camp Tate, a small camp for boys in the North Georgia mountains. The camp was staffed mainly by men associated with Georgia Tech athletics and by people from Springfield College, the

YMCA school in Massachusetts. There was a heavy emphasis on swimming and canoeing, with the Springfield contingent providing the canoeing instruction.

In August of 1935, Caldwell recalls, seven campers made a four-day canoe trip from North Georgia to Atlanta. They started on the Chestatee River and went most of the way on the Chattahoochee, which had not yet been dammed to form Lake Lanier. The only adult on the trip and the only one who had ever been on any river was Dr. Tom Cureton, a camp staff member. "He knew nothing, it turned out, of the rivers we were to travel," Caldwell relates.

The camp had a fleet of wooden, lapstrake Thompson canoes, but for some reason only two were taken on the trip. Four in a canoe, plus food and duffel! Because of numerous difficulties the group spent almost all day getting to the put-in on the Chestatee. "Dr. Cureton had recently purchased a powerful flashlight, and he suggested that we make up lost time by paddling into the night," Caldwell says. "So we put in at dusk, with Cureton and his powerful flashlight leading the way."

Things went smoothly for a while, but some time after dark the group reached a rapid. Their boats were out of control, turning round and round, and taking in water. Both canoes, however, managed to get to the left bank, where their occupants held on to bushes. Fortunately, it had been raining for several days, and the high water tended to flatten the rapid. Because of the steep bank and thick bushes it was impossible to land, and because they could hear more rapids, Cureton instructed them to tie onto the bushes and await daylight.

Caldwell remembers that summer night as the longest of his life. They couldn't stretch out in the boats and there was nothing to eat. "I never went to sleep," says Caldwell. "I vowed then never to go on another river trip. With dawn we were able to negotiate the remainder of the rapid, land, and make breakfast."

The group was met in Atlanta three days later by the driver of the camp's trusty Ford station wagon, which returned them to camp.

Caldwell did, of course, go on to make many more canoe trips during his association with summer camps. In 1952, Fritz Orr, Sr., who had operated Camp Tate since 1937, purchased Camp Merrie-Woode and that summer Caldwell made his run of the Chattooga.

During the summers of 1952 and 1953, says Caldwell, Ramone Eaton spent his vacations at Merrie-Woode and accompanied the campers on many river trips. Eaton introduced Caldwell to the beautiful Nantahala River after camp in 1952. "We used to refer to Ray as the 'Great White Father of White Waters'—partly because he was such a superb canoeist, but mainly because he had been scouting southern rivers since the late 1920s," says Caldwell.

Frank Bell described Ramone Eaton as the best paddler he'd ever met. Bell believes that Eaton made first descents on many rivers of the Southern Appalachians. It was Eaton who'd introduced him, too, to the Nantahala River in the late forties and to the Chattooga in the early fifties; he believes Eaton was probably the first to run the Nantahala. Randy Carter, a companion of Eaton's on many early runs, included descriptions of ten rivers of the Carolina Appalachians in the third edition of his classic 1967 guidebook, *Canoeing White Water: River Guide.*[1]

In addition to the North Carolina camps, which had unusually strong whitewater programs, there were many other camps doing whitewater trips

Ramone Eaton running North Carolina's Nantahala Falls in the late 1950s.
Eaton had been scouting and running Southern rivers since the 1920s, and
may have been the first to run the Nantahala. Photo courtesy of Eve H. Burton.

and training new canoeists. Both Bob Benner and I began our whitewater paddling as counselors at the Atlanta YMCA's Camp Pioneer in the mountains of North Georgia. There Hub Dowis, an Atlanta school teacher, led a canoeing and tripping program for many years. In 1951 I made a three-day, 73-mile canoe trip led by Hub on the Chattahoochee River from the vicinity of Clarkesville, Georgia, to the Roswell Road bridge outside of Atlanta. I suspect Hub knew the river well. At the time of our trip, Georgia's Buford Dam had not yet been built and I recall portaging a breached mill dam that is now covered by Lake Lanier and which several of us wanted to try running. I also remember losing several hours' paddling time one afternoon while we stopped to make repairs to one of the cedar and canvas canoes—it had been damaged by hitting a rock in a way that we would have thought little about had we been in one of today's plastic boats. Use of the wooden canoes placed a premium on attempting only those rapids that you were confident you could run successfully.

Like many other "old-time" paddlers I have run

Author Payson Kennedy, left, and Ramone Eaton, 1979. Two generations of Southern whitewater enthusiasts. Photo by Eve H. Burton.

a number of small streams which, as far as I know, had not been paddled previously. The only one that is memorable is Silvermine Creek. Those who have been to the Nantahala may remember it as the small stream entering the river at the Nantahala Outdoor Center, which can normally be walked across without getting your feet wet.

During the winter of 1972–73, our first at the Nantahala Outdoor Center, the rains came in January in a way that made me consider the advisability of starting work on an ark. My recollection is that we got 17 inches during the month. We were living in the motel on the bank of the Silvermine Creek and listened to the creek's roar through the night as it rose out of its banks. Finally one morning my daughter Frances and I decided it was runnable. It was a short run beginning below the campground and ending at the

Nantahala. So far as I know it hasn't been repeated. Hazards included low bridges, downed trees, briars, barbed-wire fences, and one outhouse extending over the stream. The turn into the culverts under Highway 19 proved the most difficult challenge of the morning and we left one kayak wrapped around the concrete. So much for personal river exploration.

Bob Benner, a founder of the Carolina Canoe Club and author of *Carolina Whitewater*,[2] made a number of first descents of lesser-known creeks and rivers of the Carolinas as he scouted streams for inclusion in his guidebooks. Ray McLeod, who accompanied Benner on several scouting trips, suggests that Benner is thought to have made first descents of the Doe River, Big Laurel Creek, and Wilson's Creek among others.

Another name that deserves mention here is

Walter Burmeister, whose guidebook *Appalachian Waters* was published in 1962.[3] The original two-volume edition covered more than 200 rivers of the Appalachians. Volume Two includes descriptions of approximately 60 rivers of the Southern Appalachian region. Amazingly, Burmeister described not just the popular whitewater runs but their entire navigable length, a truly monumental effort. In an *American Whitewater* article in 1960, Burmeister says that he began his scouting trips in 1939 and spent 20 years scouting and compiling river descriptions.[4] I suspect that he and his single foldboat made many first descents.

On the western side of the mountains summer camps played a less prominent role in early canoeing, and river running may therefore have developed somewhat later. Reid Gryder of the East Tennessee White Water Club (ETWWC) in Oak Ridge reports that the earliest runs were made by John Bombay and members of the club. Bombay was a California kayaker and safety chairman of the American Whitewater Affiliation who moved to Oak Ridge (the site of atomic energy research, the Manhattan Project) and organized the ETWWC about 1961. In his safety column in the summer 1962 issue of *American Whitewater*, he commented that so far he'd met mainly "canoeists with little boating experience . . . the ones that have most need for our safety column" and had "discovered that most canoeists out here in Tennessee had never heard of a decked canoe."[5]

In the same issue, Bombay described an exploratory trip on the South Fork of the Cumberland River with two members of the newly formed ETWWC.[6] In the winter 1962/63 issue, Bombay describes a trip on the French Broad with three professors from the University of Tennessee. His description of Frank Bell's Rapid, which may have been the rapid of Bell's memorable swim and which has become a favorite play spot for local boaters, provides an interesting indication of the changing skill levels in the 25 years since Bombay wrote. He rates it as a Class VI and says:

> When approaching Hot Springs, the roar of a cascading waterfall will become noticeable. The drop here is approximately 20 feet over a distance of 50 feet in four irregular stages. I studied this fall and found it could be run by a *very* expert boater—some world-champion white-water rat.[7]

Today, on Nantahala Outdoor Center guided trips, we sometimes take first-time paddlers through that rapid in inflatable kayaks.

River exploration prior to World War II was limited by the relative fragility and expense of the cedar and canvas canoes used. Even though the wooden canoe was actually tougher than many folks believe, it definitely couldn't take the abuse to which many of today's outstanding paddlers subject their plastic boats. Venturing onto an unknown mountain stream in a wooden canoe would give one reason to pause and reflect. With the advent and quick acceptance of the cheaper and tougher aluminum canoes, river exploration rapidly increased.

Not until the late sixties and early seventies did kayaks and decked canoes become common. During the fifties and sixties many of the lesser-known streams of the southern mountains were explored.

At the same time, communication between paddlers broadened dramatically. *American Whitewater* began publication in 1955 and was received by a growing number of Southern paddlers. The East Tennessee White Water Club was followed by the Georgia Canoeing Association in 1967. By 1972 nine whitewater clubs were listed as American Whitewater Affiliates and a large proportion of whitewater paddlers were acquainted and exchanging river information.

By the seventies and eighties the only remaining unrun streams were a few of the smaller and steeper creeks which in most cases can be run only at unusually high water levels.

NOTES

1. Randy Carter, *Canoeing White Water: River Guide* (Oakton, Va.: Appalachian Outfitters, 1967).

2. Bob Benner, *Carolina Whitewater* 4th edition (Hillsborough, N.C.: Menasha Ridge Press, 1981).

3. Walter Burmeister, *Appalachian Waters* (Washington D.C.: "Published privately by members of the Canoe Cruisers Association, Washington, D.C.," 1962).

4. Burmeister, "Saga of a Guidebook," *American Whitewater* (Vol. V, No. 4): 35–38.

5. John Bombay, *American Whitewater* (Vol. VIII, No. 1): 27.

6. Bombay, "Pioneering a *Tennessee* River," ibid: 7–8.

7. Bombay, "River Reports: The French Broad," *American Whitewater*, Vol. VIII, No. 3; 27

The author would like to gratefully acknowledge the assistance of Peter Julius in researching this article, as well as the contributions of several old-time paddlers, particularly Frank Bell and Hugh Caldwell.

KOBUK SOLO

By Jeff Rennicke   Illustrated by Lisa Derrer

Suddenly, the way that water flows in behind a stone tossed in the river, the floatplane that dropped me here drones off over the ridge to the southwest and the silence flows back in. I am alone in the Arctic.

I have forgotten the silence; I always do. It is like a bird's song just on the edge of hearing and too sweet and sad to be remembered fully. Even with the grizzlies, the caribou, and the wolf, one of Alaska's greatest natural resources is its silence. Here, it is as much a part of the landscape as wind or rock.

And I come into it gladly. I have come to this place to hear the silence again. Too many seasons guiding, smiling, telling the same stories around the campfire, playing the same songs on the guitar. It has been years since I've heard a river flow unbroken for days. So I've come here, to the headwaters to start again.

In all the years I've been running rivers in North America, I can count on one hand the number of trips that began at the beginning, the headwa-ters. Most trips begin wherever the first road happens to nudge up against the river, at the most convenient place and surrounded by sheet metal outhouses and signboards leafed in regulation forms. Running only sections of the river is like listening to scattered notes ripped from a song. This time, I want to hear the whole tune. There is a single caribou splashing in the water along the shore—once, twice and then it falls silent.

The river, which is on the western edge of the Gates of the Arctic National Park in northern Alaska, begins where that first tug of current pulls my kayak out of Walker Lake. I paddle hard once and stop. The kayak catches the current and drifts. The Kobuk River is born. Below, a school of grayling has gathered to feed at the outlet. In the clear water, they are as bright as polished stones.

I can't help thinking of the way the pilot shook my hand twice and with a little too much cere-mony, as if he never planned on seeing me again. "Solo," he kept saying, shaking his head like he

had water in his ear. I smile at the thought of him flying now somewhere over the ridge, still shaking his head.

Drifting quietly, listening for the roar of the rapid we scouted from the plane, I round a bend to find a cow moose with triplet calves feeding at midstream. The young calves, soaked from the river and glistening in the sun, are the color of polished wood and have not yet mastered the workings of their long, spindly legs. Twice, one of the calves flounders as the cow leads them out of the river. As the bow of my kayak touches shore for the scout, the moose vanish into the brush. There are grizzly tracks in the wet sand.

The Upper Kobuk Canyon rapid is just a flexing of the river's muscle really—a short stretch of small ripples that cuts left and builds into some wild Class III drops and holes. Standing above it on a rock so dark it is the color of a starless sky, there is no clear route to be seen. Several of the holes look ragged enough to be trouble but the

tail waves look inviting. Still, I am solo and every solo trip, no matter how many times you've paddled the river, is a first descent. So I compromise, portaging the gut of the rapid and riding out the tail waves below, playing once in a wave that pulses as if with a heartbeat.

Turning out of the hole finally, I pass a rock with a snapped kayak paddle jammed in a crack, its edges ragged as a broken bone. Suddenly the water seems colder and the rocks sharper and the decision to portage a little wiser.

The motion of the river against its banks seems almost hypnotic—the sun, the soft sounds of water, the silence as I sit still as stone listening for my own heartbeat. The silence washes over me like wind. I lay the paddle across the bow, lean back and drift, alone.

Suddenly, I am not alone. A wolf slides over a cutbank on the left shore, steps to the river and drinks. Its fur is a tangle of gray streaked with silver, the color of summer storm clouds, and as it steps to the river's edge its reflection rises from the still water to meet it. I paddle once to turn the bow and then freeze, watching.

Once, the wolf looks up, puzzled, looking directly at me. The kayak drifts to within 20 yards. The wolf turns and trots downstream at about the speed of the river. I drift closer: 15 yards.

The animal moves with the grace of water, smooth and supple. I can see the muscles strapped across its back rippling beneath its thin summer fur with each step. As it crosses a broad, flat rock, I hear the cut of its claws against the stone. I drift closer: 10 yards.

It stops to check a scent at a driftlog. A bolt of sunlight flashes off my paddle and the wolf is gone. Just like that, I am alone again.

This far north the sun never sets in summer; the days flow together as easily as creeks come to the river and give time a feeling of endlessness, of suspension. All the signs are here; the shadows grow long, the air goes still and cool, the light gets heavy and the nightbirds call, but the sun just circles the sky endlessly like a wanderer looking for a home. I give in to its lack of rhythm, paddling when the weather is good or when I feel a restlessness, sitting for hours on the bank memorizing cloud patterns or looking for pieces of jade on the gravel bars. I paddle most when the sun is low, it's late, and when I, like the sun, am looking for a place to rest.

It is on one of these late-night paddles, under light the color of honey, that I come into the Lower Kobuk Canyon. From out of nowhere black walls rise up like a hand closing in a fist on the river, and the air hums with the sound of rapids. An osprey is circling overhead, its sharp call slicing through even the roar of the rapids.

This is what I've come for, a dreamlike run

playing in the holes alone with no rush to move on, no designated campsites. Only the flow of the river, the light that turns the waves to splashes of diamonds as my paddle flashes through. There is in light and water a common bond and, in between, a single, solo kayak playing, forever playing. The osprey is still circling overhead, calling. There is a light in its feathers like lightning.

I awake with a start. A raven just overhead makes a sound like cracking rock and then flaps off downstream. I have fallen asleep on a hillside overlooking the confluence of the Pah and the Kobuk, in a quiet patch of cottonwood. There, among the shadows from the trees, are a pair of weather-beaten shacks, shoulder high and quiet: Eskimo grave huts. The wind in the leaves sounds like distant voices.

There is a perception of Alaska as an unbroken and unbreakable wilderness, endless. Some of it still is, but much of this land carries a long human history, a history that has not always left tracks any deeper than footprints on a riverbank or the split branches of spruce used as a tent frame, but a history just the same.

Archaeologists believe that the Kobuk Valley may have been the gateway to this continent for nomadic hunters crossing the Bering land bridge. Downstream, at Onion Portage, is one of the oldest known sites of human habitation in North America. The footprints here are ancient and the history unbroken.

The people at the villages downstream—Kobuk, Shugnak, Ambler—know this river as intimately as the pattern of beads sewn on their winter parkas, and I drift past their fish camps, abandoned until the fall salmon runs, the split spruce drying racks stained dark with the blood of generations of salmon.

The village of Kobuk is nothing but a cluster of

government houses and a few old log cabins over-looking the right bank of the river, two small stores and an immense government-provided post office painted bright red and sporting a huge radio dish out back next to a skin-drying rack. A gravel runway, the only way in or out of town besides the river, cuts just behind the post office. At the sound of each plane, the children gather to write notes in the dust on the belly of the plane to be read by the children of the next isolated village.

As I wait for the plane, I cut up salmon with an old woman on the shore. Her hands seem as bent and dark as slabs of driftwood yet she handles her *ulu*, the traditional Eskimo rounded knife, with grace and speed, cutting two fish for each one of mine. A long time ago, she tells me, she paddled the Kobuk in an *umiak*, a skin kayak. She makes a paddling motion with her hands, throwing her head back in laughter. "Now, my fat would sink the boat," she laughs, a dry, soft sound like sticks cracking.

We cut on in silence for more than a half hour until finally she asks, "Did you paddle all alone?" I hesitate, thinking of the broken kayak paddle, of the wolf, of the grave huts where the trees talk in quiet voices, and of the people who for thousands of years have cut up salmon just like this on the banks of this river. For just a moment, staring into her ancient eyes, I am not quite sure how to answer.

KOBUK RIVER, ALASKA

158

ABOUT THE EDITORS

Peripatetic, aquatic bon vivant **Cameron O'Connor** began kayaking on the Chaleau River in central France. She has participated in paddling expeditions to Chile, Peru, India, and the Northwest Territories. She now lives in Marshfield, Vermont, where she is an avid armchair adventurer.

John Lazenby's interest in rivers and boats began when he was growing up along the Susquehanna River in Pennsylvania. He is a journalist who lives in Montpelier, Vermont, where he is an editor at *Vermont Life* magazine.

ABOUT THE CONTRIBUTORS

Richard Bangs, also known as the Indiana Jones of the adventure-travel business, is the president and co-founder of Sobek Expeditions in Oakland, California. Since 1973, when he made the first descent of the Omo River in Ethiopia, Bangs has orchestrated and led more than 30 major first descents in every corner of the world. He is the co-author of *Rivergods* and is currently working on a variety of film projects.

Yvon Chouinard can frequently be found on the river, either fly fishing or kayaking . . . that is, when he is not climbing, surfing, skiing, or breaking new barriers in the outdoor equipment business. Chouinard divides his time between Ventura, California, and Moose, Wyoming, as well as a few other remote spots.

When **Whit Deschner** is not living off the tailgate of a truck or in the bilge of a gillnetter, he works on his favorite top secret project: a neutron bomb that will selectively wipe out all politicians, insurance salesmen, yuppies, babies, 15-year-olds, poodles, most rafters, '53 Oldsmobiles and a stop sign 21 miles out of Baker, Oregon, that is of extreme annoyance to him.

Timothy Hillmer is a graduate of Southern Illinois University. For eight years he worked as a river guide in California, Oregon, and Colorado. His fiction, poetry, and articles have appeared in numerous publications, and in 1987 he won first prize in the *Westword* magazine fiction contest. He is a school teacher in Louisville, Colorado.

Payson Kennedy began canoeing 47 years ago at a summer camp in the North Georgia mountains and later became a founder and leader of the Georgia Canoeing Association. In 1972 he helped found North Carolina's Nantahala Outdoor Center, where he is chairman of the board. He was also founder and first president of the association of Eastern Professional River Outfitters. Payson has won several titles in the National Open Whitewater Championships and has led numerous river trips for the NOC in Central America and Nepal.

Franz Lidz is a staff writer for *Sports Illustrated* who lives in Philadelphia with his wife, Maggie, and daughters, Gogo and Daisy Daisy. He recently bought a rowing machine and is working on a family autobiography, *Unstrung Heroes*, for Random House.

Bill Mason (1929–1988) was one of Canada's most celebrated outdoor filmmakers. Artist, author, environmentalist, hockey player and canoeist, Mason shared his love of rivers and the wilderness with all who knew him. His numerous films and books portray his sensitivity and his enthusiasm for life. His sense of humor and ever-present smile will be missed by all.

Jamie McEwan is best known for his bronze medal for C-1 slalom in the 1972 Olympics. He still races competitively and won a silver medal in the 1987 World Championships for C-2. McEwan lives with his wife, Sandra Boynton, in Lakeville, Connecticut, and recently completed a children's book.

William (never Bill) Nealy is the master cartoon artist at Menasha Ridge Press and the author of numerous whitewater books, including *KAYAK*. He lives in Hillsborough, North Carolina. When not on the river, he can usually be found lurking in the state's north-central Piedmont region.

Andrzej Pietowski left his native Poland in 1979 in search of wild rivers in Argentina. The outing, which was sponsored by the University of Cracow Kayak Club, turned into a two-year journey and a career in adventure travel. He is one of the cofounders of CANOANDES, a Manhattan-based firm that specializes in South American adventure trips.

Robert Portman and **Dan Reicher** caught kayak fever at Dartmouth College, where they were members of the Ledyard Canoe Club. In 1977 they were part of a Ledyard-sponsored kayak expedition that was the first group on record to navigate the 1,888-mile Rio Grande. Both are attorneys. Rob is in private practice in Cincinnati. Dan is on the staff of the Natural Resources Defense Council in Washington, D.C.

Jeff Rennicke is a contributing editor for *Canoe* magazine. He has traveled extensively in Alaska and Canada's north country by raft, canoe, and kayak. He lives with his wife in Boulder, Colorado.

Royal Robbins is known as one of the most outstanding and articulate climbers in North America, noted for his solo ascent of El Capitan in 1967. In the late seventies, Robbins began kayaking and has since pioneered numerous first descents in California and Chile. He is the president of Royal Robbins, a multimillion dollar company that makes and sells stylish outdoor wear.

David Roberts discovered his fear of moving water at the age of two when his mother first subjected him to a shampoo. He normally writes about drier pursuits like mountain climbing and recently finished a biography of writer Jean Stafford, published by Little, Brown.

Galen Rowell is one of America's foremost outdoor photographers and the author of numerous books, including *In the Throne Room of the Mountain Gods*. He lives in Albany, California, with his wife, Barbara.

William G. Scheller paddles where few dare to float: in urban waters. He and partner Chris Maynard were described in *The New Yorker* as the Lewis and Clark of urban canoeing. Scheller is a travel writer who lives in Newbury, Massachusetts.

Bo and Kathy Shelby met while kayaking and have since paddled rivers all over the world. They live in Corvallis, Oregon, where she is an electrical engineer with Hewlett-Packard and he is a professor of forestry at Oregon State University. They have one child, Kaitlin McKenzie Shelby, named after Oregon's McKenzie River.

Peter N. Skinner is chief environmental engineer for the office of the attorney general of the state of New York in Albany, New York. His avid pursuit of river running has led him to rivers from Alaska to Chile. His zeal for paddling is matched only by his dedication to saving free-flowing rivers.

Chuck Stanley was the U.S. slalom champion in 1980 and has been in the forefront of running first descents in California for more than a decade. He is the author of *A Guide To the Best Whitewater in the State of California.*

Scott Thybony, former river guide and park-service boatman, has lost count of the number of times he ran the Colorado River. That's why he's a writer and not a mathematician. His stories have appeared in *Outside, National Wildlife,* and various National Geographic Society publications.

OTHER MENASHA RIDGE PRESS BOOKS

A Hiking Guide to the Trails of Florida, Elizabeth F. Carter

The Squirt Book: The Manual of Squirt Kayaking Technique, James E. Snyder, illustrated by W. Nealy

Chattooga River (Section IV) Flip Map, Ron Rathnow

Nantahala River Flip Map, Ron Rathnow

New River Flip Map, Ron Rathnow

Ocoee River Flip Map, Ron Rathnow

Youghiogheny River Flip Map, Ron Rathnow

Kayak: The Animated Manual of Intermediate and Advanced Whitewater Technique, William Nealy

Kayaks to Hell, William Nealy

Whitewater Home Companion, Southeastern Rivers, Volume I, William Nealy

Whitewater Home Companion, Southeastern Rivers, Volume II, William Nealy

Whitewater Tales of Terror, William Nealy

Carolina Whitewater: A Canoeist's Guide to the Western Carolinas, Bob Benner

A Paddler's Guide to Eastern North Carolina, Bob Benner and Tom McCloud

Wildwater West Virginia, Volume I, The Northern Streams, Paul Davidson, Ward Eister, and Dirk Davidson

Wildwater West Virginia, Volume II, The Southern Streams, Paul Davidson, Ward Eister, and Dirk Davidson

Diver's Guide to Underwater America, Kate Kelley and John Shobe

Shipwrecks: Diving the Graveyard of the Atlantic, Roderick M. Farb

Boatbuilder's Manual, Charles Walbridge, editor

Smoky Mountains Trout Fishing Guide, Don Kirk

Fishing the Great Lakes of the South: An Angler's Guide to the TVA System, Don and Joann Kirk

A Fishing Guide to Kentucky's Major Lakes, Arthur B. Lander, Jr.

A Guide to the Backpacking and Day-Hiking Trails of Kentucky, Arthur B. Lander, Jr.

A Canoeing and Kayaking Guide to the Streams of Florida, Volume I, North Central Peninsula and Panhandle, Elizabeth F. Carter and John L. Pearce

A Canoeing and Kayaking Guide to the Streams of Florida, Volume II, Central and South Peninsula, Lou Glaros and Doug Sphar

Appalachian Whitewater, Volume I, The Southern Mountains, Bob Sehlinger, Don Otey, Bob Benner, William Nealy, and Bob Lantz

Appalachian Whitewater, Volume II, The Central Mountains, Ed Grove, Bill Kirby, Charles Walbridge, Ward Eister, Paul Davidson, and Dirk Davidson

Appalachian Whitewater, Volume III, The Northern Mountains, John Connelly and John Porterfield

Northern Georgia Canoeing, Bob Sehlinger and Don Otey

Southern Georgia Canoeing, Bob Sehlinger and Don Otey

A Canoeing and Kayaking Guide to the Streams of Kentucky, Bob Sehlinger

A Canoeing and Kayaking Guide to the Streams of Ohio, Volume I, Richard Combs and Stephen E. Gillen

A Canoeing and Kayaking Guide to the Streams of Ohio, Volume II, Richard Combs and Stephen E. Gillen

A Canoeing and Kayaking Guide to the Streams of Tennessee, Volume I, Bob Sehlinger and Bob Lantz

A Canoeing and Kayaking Guide to the Streams of Tennessee, Volume II, Bob Sehlinger and Bob Lantz

Emergency Medical Procedures for the Outdoors, Patient Care Publications, Inc.

Guide and Map to the Uwharrie Trail, G. Nicholas Hancock

Harsh Weather Camping, Sam Curtis

Modern Outdoor Survival, Dwight R. Schuh